STUDIES IN HISTORY, ECONOMICS AND PUBLIC LAW

Edited by the

FACULTY OF POLITICAL SCIENCE
OF COLUMBIA UNIVERSITY

―――――

NUMBER 396

DISSOLUTION OF THE BRITISH PARLIAMENT

1832–1931

BY

CHI KAO WANG

DISSOLUTION OF THE BRITISH PARLIAMENT

1832–1931

BY

CHI KAO WANG

AMS PRESS

NEW YORK

COLUMBIA UNIVERSITY
STUDIES IN THE
SOCIAL SCIENCES

396

The series was formerly known as
Studies in History, Economics and Public Law.

Reprinted with the permission of Columbia University Press
From the edition of 1934, New York
First AMS EDITION published 1970
Manufactured in the United States of America

Library of Congress Catalog Card Number: 75-120206
International Standard Book Number:
    Complete Set: 0-404-51000-0
    Number 396: 0-404-51396-4

A M S PRESS, INC.
New York, N.Y. 10003

PREFACE

MINISTERIAL responsibility is differently conceived of by differing political scientists, variously prescribed by the constitutions which accept the principle, and vagariously applied by those who hold office. For the successful working out of the doctrine it is generally agreed that there must be a complementary power of dissolution.

In the United States, where a rigid system of separation of powers is maintained, the executive has no responsibility to the legislature and the Congress is not subject to dissolution by the President or the Cabinet. In Switzerland, the collegial executive, although elected by the Federal Assembly, is not responsible to it, while the term of the Federal Assembly may not be curtailed by dissolution, except in case of total revision of the constitution, which is now highly unlikely to occur. In pre-war Germany the Cabinet was responsible not to the Reichstag but to the Kaiser, through whose ordinance, issued with the consent of the Bundesrat, the Reichstag could be brought to an end. The Weimar Constitution of 1919, totally discarded by Hitler since his appointment to the Chancellorship in January, 1933, expressly made the Cabinet responsible to the Reichstag but it also invested in the President of the Reich the power of dissolution. So long as the President had some discretion in respect of dismissing the ministry and refusing or ordering dissolution, the establishment of complete ministerial responsibility, in the English sense, was impossible. In France the Chamber of Deputies may be dissolved by the President with the consent of the Senate. Since 1877, however, convention has worked against the practice so that the ministry, while responsible, has practically no power to dis-

5

solve the Chamber of Deputies. Only in the English system has there always existed, though to a less extent now than in the past, a constitutional equilibrium between ministerial responsibility to the House of Commons in respect of legislation and policy, and the prerogative, exercised by the Cabinet, of dissolving the legislative assembly. The equilibrium is now disturbed in the direction of less responsibility. The counterweight of dissolution is made to weigh too heavily. What Walter Bagehot called " the regulator " of the British Constitution nowadays perhaps regulates too much. The Cabinet is less than formerly the creature of the House of Commons, and this because of its power to destroy its own creator.

The purpose of this monograph is to deal not so much with the theory justifying a " regulator " for a parliamentary machine as to describe in some detail the use of the power during the past century. On the basis of the evidence, I have attempted a few generalizations, but no one realizes more clearly than I do that they are few and tentative. For them to be otherwise, I would have had to write another monograph, reanalyzing the data I present, and checking it with evidence drawn from party rather than parliamentary and biographical sources. Generalizations further than those I attempt I leave to others and trust that my monograph will at least give them a more adequate factual background than has been available to earlier generalizers.

Dissolutions which took place before the Reform Bill of 1832 have been dealt with briefly by way of introduction. Emphasis is laid on dissolutions since that memorable date, not because the earlier dissolutions of an unreformed House of Commons were not interesting and important but because, since 1832, dissolutions have been more intimately tied to the developing doctrine of ministerial responsibility for legislation.

This matter receives rather extensive consideration in the three chapters following the introduction. In Chapter V, I have discussed resignation of the ministry and dissolution of Parliament as the alternatives confronting the government when it is defeated in the House of Commons, and I have examined the criteria which have dictated the choice of one alternative in preference to the other. The changed relation between the Cabinet and the House of Commons as a result *inter alia* of the increasing power and elaborateness of party organizations, the large extensions of the suffrage and the emergence of the theory of the mandate, have been dealt with so that recent controversies as to constitutional significance of the power of dissolution may be examined.

I wish to express my thanks to Professor Lindsay Rogers not only for some of his ideas, which he will trust I have been able to improve upon, but also for assistance during the preparation and completion of the work. I am deeply indebted also to Professor Robert Livingston Schuyler who read the manuscript and made invaluable suggestions. My profound gratitude is due to Dr. Thomas P. Peardon who has furnished valuable advice and criticism with regard to particular portions of the work and helped me in putting it in its present form. The expert attention of Mrs. Cecil P. Killien has greatly lessened the number of stylistic vagaries.

In no case, however, do they share the responsibility for errors or defects that may appear in this monograph.

C. K. W.

November, 1933, New York City.

TABLE OF CONTENTS

9

CHAPTER I

HISTORICAL INTRODUCTION

DURING a long period of English history there were recurrent disputes between King and Parliament on the subject of the frequency with which Parliament ought to be summoned. As far back as 1311, the statutory obligation was imposed on the king that he should " hold a Parliament once in the year, or twice, if need be;[1] but such a provision was not strictly enforced.[2] The Triennial Act, 1641, passed in the early days of the Long Parliament, provided that the interval between parliaments should not be longer than three years, and the very process of summoning parliament was made independent of the king.[3] This act was repealed as

---

[1] The New Ordinances, 1311, Adams and Stephens, *Select Documents of English Constitutional History* (New York, 1901), p. 95.

[2] In Edward I's reign Parliament used to meet thrice a year. " The three sessions a year of Edward I's time are reduced to about three in two years in Edward II's, to one a year in the middle of the fourteenth century, and in the fifteenth century to one in two, three, four, or even five years. This progressive rarity of Parliaments is not due to the tyranny of kings, for it proceeds independently of the dynasty or particular monarch; it is due to a fundamental change in the character of parliament, to the specialization of functions previously performed by a rudimentary organ, and to the transference of most of the original work of parliament to the council and to chancery." In other words, it is due to " the loss of original functions through the transformation of parliament from a high court into a legislature." Pollard, *The Evolution of Parliament* (London, 1926), pp. 130-132.

[3] The elaborate machinery provided was that if the king did not issue the appropriate summons when due, a Parliament was to be elected and to meet without his intervention. The obligation to issue the necessary writs of election to the boroughs, cities, counties, etc., " without any further warrant or direction from His Majesty, his heirs, or successors "

" in derogation of his Majesty's just right and prerogative " by the Triennial Act of 1664, which, however, again declared that " the sitting and holding of parliaments shall not be intermitted or discontinued above three years at the most." Since no sanction was attached to this provision, it was ignored both by Charles II and by James II.[4] Indeed until the Revolution of 1688 the occurrence of long periods of government without a Parliament constituted a characteristic

was to be first devolved on the Lord Chancellor and the Lord Keeper of the Seal, and failing that, on any twelve peers, and then on sheriffs, and finally, on the freeholders of the counties, the masters and scholars of the universities, and the citizens and others having suffrage rights. This provision of the Triennial Act of 1641, which was abolished in 1664, was a deviation from the ancient rule of the English Constitution that no Parliament can meet except on royal summons; but actually it was never put into operation. Historically the assembly of Lords and Commons, which met in 1660 to restore the exiled Charles, was not summoned by royal writs. This technical difficulty was obviated by the device of passing a statute after the King's return " for removing and preventing all questions and disputes concerning the assembling and sitting of this present parliament." A similar plan was adopted in 1689 to give an appearance of formal legality to the Convention Parliament which displaced James II and installed William and Mary on the throne.

According to Professor D. O. Dykes of the University of Edinburgh, the only exception to this ancient rule is that " upon the demise of the Crown the Parliament (formerly automatically dissolved) shall survive for six months (a limit now abolished by Reform Act, 1867) and shall meet without a summons (7 & 8 Wm. III, cap. 15; re-enacted 6 Anne, cap. 7). Moreover, by the Meeting of Parliament Act, 1797 (37 Geo. III, cap. 127) a dissolved Parliament, when a new one has not been constituted, is revived on the like occasion and meets without a summons." Dykes, *Source Book of Constitutional History from 1660* (London, 1930), pp. 3, 19.

[4] Parliament was not assembled during the last four years of the reign of Charles II. After the accession of James II it was formally prorogued on November 30, 1685. Dissolution did not follow until July, 1687, but Parliament did not meet and no general election was held between November, 1685, and the departure ot James on December 23, 1688. *Cf.* Hallam, *Constitutional History of England* (London, 1832), vol. iii, pp. 79-83 and Green, *Short History of the English People* (N. Y., 2nd ed.), pp. 663-682.

grievance against the Stuart regime. The Bill of Rights of 1689 merely stated that "parliaments ought to be held frequently." But the annual session of Parliament was made necessary by two other clauses of the Bill of Rights which required Parliament to vote the money for the maintenance of the administration and to grant sanction to the standing army " for one year only." Consequently, since 1689, no year has passed without a Parliamentary session.[5]

The Triennial Act of 1694 dealt both with the frequency and with the duration of Parliaments. While providing that Parliament should be "holden once in three years at the least," [6] it further stipulated that "no parliament shall have any continuance longer than three years only." The potential life of a Parliament, limited by this act to three years was lengthened in 1716 by the Septennial Act to seven years. The latter act (which was of course a striking illustration of the sovereignty of Parliament) was passed in order to avoid the necessity of an election in 1717 at a time when Jacobite feeling in the country seemed to have reached a high point. So far as we are concerned, "the real effect of the measure was to produce a great irregularity in the duration of Parliaments, and the times of holding elections." [7] From 1716 on, the Crown was to have greater discretion in deciding whether a Parliament should be dissolved and a general election should be held. The maximum duration of Parliaments remained at seven years until the Parliament Act of 1911 enacted that "five years shall be substituted for seven years . . . under the Septennial Act." The shortening of the parliamentary duration in 1911 was an "obvious concession

---

[5] Dykes, *op. cit.,* pp. 15-17.

[6] According to law, the king even now need not summon Parliament oftener than once in three years.

[7] J. G. Randall. "The Frequency and Duration of Parliaments," *American Political Science Review,* vol. x, no. 4, November, 1916.

which the Asquith Government offered as a sort of palliative against the drastic provisions of the Parliament Bill." [8] Through more frequent dissolutions of Parliament, the electorate would be made more effective as a check against the legal omnipotence of the House of Commons.

Apart from being regulated by law, the existence of Parliament used to be affected by the demise of the Crown. In the early period of English history, the King summoned, by writ, the three estates of the realm to appear in person, or by their representatives, to advise, assent, or enact. " It was natural," as Sir William Anson said, " that the invitation should lapse and the assembly disperse when he who summoned it had died; for the medieval Parliaments came together, not so much because the people wanted to take part in public affairs, as because the King wanted money and information; and the theory that Parliament owed its existence to the King's writ was true to this extent, that the writ was the recognized means by which the three estates could be brought together." [9]   Though the theory regarding dissolution of Parliament in case of the demise of the Crown was not unreasonable, the practice was evidently inconvenient. The inconvenience was met by an Act of Parliament passed in 1696 (7 & 8 Will. III, c. 15; re-enacted 6 Anne c. 7 in 1707) which provided that the Parliament in existence at the king's demise should continue in existence for six months but no longer after his death, " unless sooner prorogued or dissolved by " his successor. It further provided that in case there should be no parliament in being, at the time of the demise of the king, " then the last preceding parliament shall immediately convene and sit, and is . . . impowered and required to act as aforesaid, to all intents and purposes, as

[8] *Ibid.*

[9] Anson, *The Law and Custom of the Constitution*, vol. i (4th ed., Oxford, 1909), pp. 73-74.

if the said parliament had never been dissolved." The six months limitation was finally removed by the Reform Act of 1867, so that since that time the existence of Parliament has been unaffected by the death of the king.[10]

Because of the fact that before the Revolution there was not strict enforcement of the parliamentary acts regarding the frequency and no regulation of the duration of Parliament, a Parliament before the end of the seventeenth century remained in session only so long as the king wished. Its dissolution, except in case of a demise of the Crown, which would *ipso facto* bring a Parliament to an end, depended entirely upon the will of the king.[11] After William and

[10] The only Act concerning the existence of Parliament in case of the demise of the Crown which still remains in force is the Meeting of Parliament Act of 1797 (37 Geo. III, cap. 127), by which it was provided that if the demise of the Crown shall occur after the dissolution or expiration of one Parliament and before the date upon which the new Parliament is, by the writs, summoned to meet, then the defunct Parliament shall revive and meet, and survive, unless dissolved by the new Sovereign, for six months.

[11] The Triennial Act of 1641 (16 Car. I, c. 1), provided that no Parliament was to be dissolved or prorogued within fifty days of its meeting without the consent of the king and the two houses; but this Act, as we have said, was never put in operation and was formally repealed in 1664 by 16 Car. II, c. 1. J. G. Randall, "The Frequency and Duration of Parliaments," see *supra*, p. 13, fn. 7.

The act passed on May 11, 1641 under the title "the Act against Dissolving the Long Parliament without its own Consent" (16 Car. I, c. 7) expressly provided that "this present Parliament now assembled shall not be dissolved unless it be by Act of Parliament to be passed for that purpose; nor shall be, at any time or times, during the continuance thereof, prorogued or adjourned, unless it be by Act of Parliament to be likewise passed for that purpose; . . . and that all and every thing or things whatsoever done or to be done for the adjournment, proroguing, or dissolving of this present Parliament, contrary to this Act, shall be utterly void and of none effect." It was on the basis of this Act that John Bradshaw, the President of the Council of State, said to Cromwell as follows, after the latter had ejected the "Rump" and its executive committee, the Council of State, in April, 1653: "We have heard what you have done this morning (April 20, 1653) at the

Mary ascended the throne in 1689, however, not only was the annual session of Parliament guaranteed through the necessity of passing the Mutiny and Finance Acts every year and the maximum duration of parliaments prescribed, but the demise of the Crown as a cause of dissolution of Parliament was also regulated.

The appearance of the Cabinet in the eighteenth century and the gradual development of the idea of Cabinet responsibility wrought even greater changes than these in the exercise by the king of his prerogative regarding dissolution. The dissolution of Parliament by William III in 1701 was the last occasion when that prerogative was exercised by the sovereign except upon the advice of his ministers.[12]   Associated with this change is the fact that the early practice that dissolution was personally announced by the sovereign to the Commons, who had been called to the House of Lords for the purpose, was also abandoned by the end of the seventeenth century.   " Since 1681 the only instance of personal dissolution was in 1818, when the Prince Regent, acting for George III, adopted this course." [13]   The usual method is to prorogue Parliament, and, shortly after, to dissolve it by a Royal Proclamation which is issued by the king on the advice of the Privy Council under the Great Seal.[14]   Thus, the

House, and in some hours all England will hear it. But you mistake, Sir, if you think the Parliament dissolved. No power on earth can dissolve the Parliament but itself, be sure of that! " As a matter of fact, the Long Parliament was dissolved through a resolution passed in April, 1660 by the assembly of those members who had been excluded from the House of Commons by Pride's Purge in 1648. Green, *A Short History of the English People*, pp. 581, 600.

[12] Anson, *op. cit.*, vol. i, pp. 304-305. " The Prerogative of Dissolution," *Round Table*, vol. 20, no. 77, pp. 32-49, Dec., 1929.

[13] Redlich, *The Procedure of the House of Commons* (London, 1908), vol. ii, p. 65.

[14] In case of the expiration of the term, the dissolution of Parliament may technically come about without the exercise of the prerogative and

change in the way by which the dissolution of Parliament is proclaimed has the significant effect of transferring the responsibility for dissolution from the king to his ministers.[15]

Though some threads of the idea of Cabinet responsibility can be traced as far back as the end of the seventeenth century, the Cabinet system as we understand it now, that is, a system of government which implies the doctrines of Cabinet solidarity and collective responsibility to the majority of the House of Commons,[16] is a more modern development. Despite the momentous change in the Constitution caused by the withdrawal of the sovereign from Cabinet Councils after George I ascended the throne,[17] the king still

the issuance of the Proclamation. But no Parliament has been allowed to continue for its full term since 1716, save during the Great War, when the Parliament then in existence prolonged its life by statute until peace was declared, and that Parliament also, like all its predecessors, was finally dissolved by Royal Proclamation. MacDonagh, *The English King* (New York, 1929), p. 190.

[15] Besides discharging the existing Parliament from its duties of attendance, declaring the desire of the Crown to have the advice of its people, and the royal will and pleasure to call a new Parliament, the Royal Proclamation announces an Order addressed by the Crown in Council to the Chancellors of Great Britain and Ireland to issue the necessary writs, and states that this Proclamation is to be their authority for so doing. "The Order in Council is made by the King 'by and with the advice of his Privy Council.' Those persons who are present at the meeting of the council at which the order is made assume the responsibility for what is done." Anson, *The Law and Custom of the Constitution*, vol. ii (3rd ed., Oxford, 1907), p. 54.

[16] Among what Lord Morley called the four principal features of the English system of Cabinet government are the doctrine of collective responsibility and the doctrine that "the Cabinet is answerable immediately to the majority of the House of Commons, and ultimately to the electors whose will creates that majority." Cf. *The Works of Lord Morley* (London, 1921), vol. xiii, *Walpole*, pp. 141-4.

[17] "Queen Anne held a Cabinet every Sunday, at which she was herself present. . . . With a doubtful exception in the time of George III, no sovereign has been present at a meeting of the Cabinet since Anne, though George II presided on one memorable occasion at a meet-

retained the right to appoint and dismiss his ministers. Furthermore, "throughout the eighteenth century Cabinets were mainly composed of peers ";[18] and it was not until the latter half of the nineteenth century that the House of Lords had definitely declined to the status of what Walter Bagehot (in 1865) called "a *reservoir* of Cabinet ministers." [19]   At the beginning of the eighteenth century "impeachment . . . was still . . . regarded as the proper process against ministers who had gravely offended a triumphant majority.   It was the only way then known of securing responsibility to Parliament." [20]   Since legal responsibility, as Sir William Anson said, "could not fairly be fixed upon an entire Cabinet for the action of one of its members ",[21] it is natural that the idea of collective responsibility was probably unknown to the statesmen then.[22]   The recognition of such responsibility begins in the last twenty years of the eighteenth century. Prior to 1782, "there had been frequent instances of partial alterations in the Cabinet, with a view to conciliate the favour of Parliament, but it was not until the downfall of Lord

ing of the Privy Council, which is not easily to be distinguished from a Cabinet. . . . The withdrawal of the sovereign from Cabinet Councils was essential to the momentous change which has transferred the whole substance of authority and power from the Crown to a committee chosen by one member of the two Houses of Parliament, from among other members." *Ibid.,* p. 138.

[18] *Ibid.,* p. 136.

[19] Bagehot, *The English Constitution* (New York and London, 1927), p. 81.

[20] *The Works of Lord Morley,* vol. xiii, *Walpole,* pp. 39-41.

[21] Anson, *op. cit.,* vol. ii, pp. 107-108.

[22] "The memorable decision to create twelve peers in a day," in 1712, "was taken without reference to the body (Cabinet), whose collective assent to so momentous a step would today be regarded as not any less indispensable a preliminary than the assent of the sovereign herself (the creation took place at Queen Anne's time) ! " *The Works of Lord Morley,* vol. xiii, *Walpole,* p. 140.

North's administration, in 1782, that the necessity for a complete change in the ministry . . . was freely acknowledged." [23] Furthermore, ministerial responsibility in the modern sense, that is, responsibility to public opinion and liability to loss of office as in contrast to liability to impeachment, was also unknown to the statesmen and writers of the early part of the eighteenth century. When Montesquieu visited England in 1732, no ministry had ever resigned because of a defeat in the House of Commons; and, in fact, the enforcement of the fourth and sixth sections of the Act of Settlement, 1701 [24] (which had been repealed in 1705 by 4 Anne, c. 8), would have secured that "separation of powers" which he championed. When his *Esprit des Lois* was published in 1748, there had been but one case of resignation of a ministry (the resignation of Sir Robert Walpole in February, 1742) as a result of defeat in the House of Commons, and the principles of Cabinet responsibility were then not well understood. The House of Commons was not yet entirely conscious that the best way of enforcing ministerial responsibility was to allow no business to be done until an obnoxious minister retired, for it strove to impeach Walpole after his defeat. [25]

[23] Todd, *On Parliamentary Government in England*, vol. i (London, 1887), p. 138.

[24] The Act of Settlement provided that "all matters and things relating to the well-governing of this Kingdom which are properly cognizable in the Privy Council by the laws and customs of this Realm shall be transacted there" and also that no place-men should sit in the House of Commons. Dykes, *Source Book of Constitutional History from 1660*, p. 8; and *cf. The Works of Lord Morley*, vol. xiii, *Walpole*, pp. 128-130.

[25] Adams, *Constitutional History of England* (New York, 1921), p. 393. Lord Morley said, "the proceedings against Oxford and Bolingbroke (in 1715) are the last instance in our history of a political impeachment. They are the last ministers who were ever made personally responsible for giving bad advice and pursuing a discredited policy, and since then a political mistake has ceased to be a crime. Warren

After 1742, the only ministers before the Reform Act of 1832 who resigned in consequence of defeats in the House of Commons were Lord Shelburne in 1783 and the Duke of Wellington in 1830.[26] The defeat which drove Walpole from power took place in a committee of the House sitting to hear the election petition of Chippenham.[27] Shelburne was beaten on Lord John Cavendish's Resolution of Censure on the terms of the peace between Great Britain and America.[28] The Duke of Wellington's defeat was on a motion to refer the civil list estimates to a select committee.[29] In short, ministers before 1832 were " solely responsible for the fulfillment of their executive obligations, and for obtaining the sanction of Parliament to such measures as they deemed to be essential for carrying out their public policy ";[30] and there was no instance before the Reform of 1832 of a

Hastings was impeached (1788), and so was Lord Melville (1804), but neither case was political, for Hastings was charged with mis-government, and Melville with malversation of official funds. Burke said in 1770 that impeachment was dead, even to the very idea of it, and later history has shown that he was substantially in the right." *The Works of Lord Morley*, vol. xiii, *Walpole*, p. 40.

[26] In 1782 a direct vote of want of confidence on the North Government on the question of the recognition of American independence was negatived by a bare majority of nine in the House of Commons; but Lord Surrey gave notice of a similar motion for March 20 of the same year, which it was anticipated would pass. To forestall this defeat, the North Government resigned, and the resignation was communicated to the House of Commons on the day the debate was to have begun. Todd, *op. cit.*, vol. i, p. 139. *Cf.* further *ibid.*, vol. i, pp. 138 *et seq.*, especially the "Tabular View of the Administrations of Great Britain from 1782 to 1880," on pp. 253-258 and Emden, *The People and the Constitution* (Oxford, 1933), chapter vii, " The Choice of Ministries " and appendix iv, " Chronological Summary of Parliaments and Ministries " and appendix v, " Chart of Parliaments and Ministries ".

[27] *The Works of Lord Morley*, vol. xiii, *Walpole*, pp. 222 *et seq.*

[28] *Parliamentary History of England*, vol. 23, cols. 570-571.

[29] Todd, *op. cit.*, vol. i, p. 187.

[30] *Ibid.*, vol. ii (London, 1889), pp. 368-9.

ministry retiring because it was beaten on a question of legislation.[31] But the growing interest exhibited by the electorate and the rapid demand for great remedial measures, together with the difficulty experienced by private members in carrying bills through Parliament led to "the imposition of additional burthens upon the ministers of the crown, by requiring them to prepare and submit to Parliament whatever measures . . . may be needed for the public good; and also to take the lead in advising Parliament to amend or reject all crude, imperfect or otherwise objectionable measures . . . introduced by private members." [32] By the middle of the nineteenth century the responsibility of the ministers for legislation was recognized, and the ministers thereafter would treat the rejection of any of their important measures as equivalent to a vote of want of confidence.[33]

The prerogative of dissolution is significant chiefly because of its being exercised as what Professor Lindsay Rogers has called "the complementary power" [34] to cabinet responsibility

[31] Lord Grey's Government was defeated in April, 1831 by eight votes (299 vs. 291 votes) on General Gascoigne's Amendment to the Reform Bill in the House of Commons. Realizing, as Lord John Russell said, that "the country was ready to follow Lord Grey, and to adopt his measure as a satisfactory settlement" of the question of parliamentary reform, the government preferred an immediate dissolution of Parliament scarcely more than six months after a general election to retirement from office and abandonment of reform. Lord Russell, *Recollections and Suggestions 1813-1873* (London, 1875), pp. 74-5. This, incidentally, was the only occasion prior to 1832 upon which Parliament was dissolved on account of the defeat of the ministry in the House of Commons.

[32] Todd, *op. cit.*, vol. ii, pp. 368-369.

[33] Lowell, *The Government of England* (New York, 1919), vol. i, p. 316.

[34] McBain and Rogers, *The New Constitutions of Europe* (Garden City, N. Y., 1923), p. 30. *Cf.* Rogers, "Parliamentary Commissions in France, II", *Political Science Quarterly*, vol. 38, no. 4, Dec., 1923, esp. p. 18. Rogers, "Ministerial Instability in France", *Political Science Quarterly*, vol. 46, no. 1, March, 1931, esp. pp. 606-607.

to the House of Commons.[35] The responsibility of the
Cabinet to the House of Commons was not fully developed
until after 1832; and accordingly the dissolution power interests us mainly in its manifestations since that date. But in
order to make our study more complete it will be desirable
to explain briefly those dissolutions that did occur before
1832. Aside from the fact that before the Revolution Parliaments were dissolved by the sovereign in complete independence of ministerial advice, the king could pack the House
of Commons by creating new boroughs by charter. Though
this practice fell into desuetude after the Revolution,[36] cor-
ruption had been gaining ground ever since the time of
Charles II.[37]   As Sir Courtenay Ilbert said,[38]

throughout the eighteenth century and the early part of the nine-

[35] Ministers are responsible to the House of Commons, that is to say,
can not continue without the confidence of the House of Commons; but
the existence of the prerogative of dissolution in England gives ministers
the alternative of appeal to the people instead of resignation when the
House of Commons has in any way indicated lack of confidence. Hence
not only is the ministry held responsible to the House of Commons, but
the House of Commons is prevented from abusing its powers at the
expense of effective government by overturning ministries for frivolous
reasons or on frequent occasions.

[36] Professor Pollard said in his *The Evolution of Parliament* (pp.
323-324) that 'the creation of new boroughs was slightly, if at all, due
to the crown's desire to pack the house. Under Henry VII and Henry
VIII forty-five new members were added, under Edward VI thirty,
under Mary twenty-seven, and under Elizabeth fifty-nine. From 297
members at the accession of Henry VIII the house had grown to 458
by the death of Elizabeth". Again, he said (p. 273) that "as early
as the reign of Elizabeth the motive for new creations was rather the
political ambition of the constituency than the desire of the crown for
'king's friends' in the house of commons . . . James I created university
constituencies, but Charles II's letters patent to Newark seem to have
been the last occasion upon which the crown increased the house of
commons by charter instead of by acts of parliament."

[37] *The Works of Lord Morley*, vol. xiii, *Walpole*, p. 111.

[38] Ilbert, *Parliament* (New York and London, 1911), pp. 45-46.

teenth century seats were freely and openly bought and sold.
They were even advertised for sale, like livings in the church.
. . . Prices varied much, according to place and time, but between 1812 and 1832 the ordinary price of a seat bought for a
parliament is said to have been between £ 5,000 and £ 6,000.
The existence of this phenomenon coupled with the preval-
ence of direct bribery not only rendered the complete establishment of parliamentary responsibility impossible,[39] but also
deprived the power of dissolution of its proper significance
in the Constitution and thus led to the abuse in the exercise
of this power by the Crown. Under the electoral system
prior to the Reform in 1832, "almost any Ministry which
enjoyed the support of the Crown could," as Anson said,
" command such a majority as would enable it to hold
office." [40] In fact, " the king's choice of his advisers was
sometimes a determining factor in the membership of the
House of Commons." [41] Furthermore, the king often dissolved Parliament "on account of the existence of disputes
between the two Houses of Parliament, which have rendered
it impossible for them to work together in harmony." [42] The
only case of dissolution of Parliament which was caused by
a defeat in the House of Commons before 1832 was, as we
have pointed out,[43] the dissolution of 1831 following Lord
Grey's defeat in the lower house on the Reform Bill; and
yet this instance happened so late and it was so closely related
with the reform movement that it might be regarded as mark-
ing the dawning of a new epoch in English history rather

[39] *Cf*. Lord Rosebery, *Pitt* (London, 1919), pp. 77-78.

[40] Anson, *The Law and Custom of the Constitution,* vol. ii, pp. 131-132.

[41] As in 1695, 1701, 1702, 1710 and 1784. *Cf*. Emden, *The People and the Constitution,* pp. 141 *et seq*.

[42] As in 1679, 1701 and 1705. *Cf*. Todd, *On Parliamentary Govern- ment in England,* vol. ii, p. 505.

[43] See *supra*, p. 21, fn. 31.

than belonging to the era of " rotten boroughs " and "pocket boroughs " of the unreformed England.

Such examples show that the power of dissolution was exercised prior to 1832 not so much as a complementary power to Cabinet responsibility to the House of Commons as for other reasons. This is why, as we have already suggested, we shall lay more stress on events since than on those before the Reform of 1832. With this fact in view, we shall endeavour to analyse, in the following chapters, the various aspects of the problem of dissolution of Parliament and then to discuss its relation to ministerial responsibility to the House of Commons.

CHAPTER II

Who Dissolved the Parliaments

THE power to dissolve Parliament is a prerogative of the Crown, recognized by statute.[1] In the eyes of the law, only the sovereign, subject to certain limitations to be described later, has the right to prorogue and to dissolve Parliament. But, as we have said, since 1701, when William III exercised this prerogative in complete independence of ministerial advice, no Parliament has been dissolved by the sovereign except upon the advice of his ministers.[2] This results in the strange paradox of the Cabinet, which is " wholly unknown to the law," [3] being held responsible for the dissolution of Parliament, whereas the sovereign although legally entitled to dissolve Parliament can not, in constitutional practice, take such action without the advice of his ministers.[4]

Although Parliament may be dissolved by the sovereign only upon the advice of his ministers, yet the discretion of the ministers in rendering the advice has not always been unfettered. In 1834, when William IV dismissed Lord Melbourne from the Premiership despite the support of a majority of Parliament and summoned Sir Robert Peel to

[1] 1660, 12 Car. II, c. 1.
  1664, 16 Car. II, c. 1.
  1694, 6 & 7 Will. & Mary, c. 2.
  1696, 7 & 8 Will. III, c. 15.
  1707, 6 Anne, c. 7.
  1716, 1 Geo. I, stat. 2, c. 38.
  1867, 30 & 31 Vict., c. 102.
[2] See *supra*, p. 16, fn. 12.
[3] Ogg, *English Government and Politics* (New York, 1930), p. 119.
[4] However, no ministerial countersignature is needed in the Royal Proclamation for the dissolution of Parliament.

form a government, the latter "being absent from England, could exercise no effective control over the king's untoward precipitancy, and he found on his return (from Rome) that the military promptitude of Wellington had left him no choice but to become Prime Minister." [5] The dissolution of the existing Parliament was "practically and perhaps unavoidably decided" before Peel's return, although, as he said, he had little doubt that if upon his arrival the question of dissolution had been *res integra,* and if a perfectly free and unfettered judgment could have been formed upon it by him, he would have decided to dissolve without delay.[6]

No dismissal of the ministry by the sovereign, however, has taken place since 1834; and even should such a dismissal occur the circumstances would not be quite analogous to the unique situation existing in 1834.[7] So, the discretion of the ministry in giving advice in regard to dissolution is, in general, free and unhampered. This is especially true of a ministry supported by a majority in Parliament. The head of such a ministry can, so to speak, enforce his wishes on the sovereign, even though the latter does not accede to a dissolution. For,[8]

[5] Thursfield, *Peel* (London, 1904), pp. 144-145.

[6] *Memoirs by Sir Robert Peel* (London, 1856-7), vol. ii, pp. 43-45.

[7] Even the dismissal of Duke of Portland by George III in 1783 is not quite comparable on account of the fact that William Pitt, the successor to the Duke of Portland, was able to hold a dissolution in reserve while he attempted to secure the support of the existing Parliament, whereas in 1834 Sir Robert Peel, on his return to England, "found matters already in such a train that it was impossible for him to recede and equally impossible for him to postpone a dissolution." Thursfield, *op. cit.,* pp. 144-145.

[8] Strachey, "A Minority Premier," *Spectator,* vol. 131, p. 1020, December 29, 1923.

This is what Lord Salisbury thought would happen in 1886, if Queen Victoria should refuse a dissolution when asked for by Mr. Gladstone after his defeat on his Home Rule Bill. *Letters of Queen Victoria, 1886-1901* (New York, 1930-1932), vol. i, pp. 128-130.

if the King refuses a dissolution to a Majority Premier, the Premier resigns. But that will not prevent a dissolution, for the leader of the Opposition, when sent for by the King, will be obliged, save in an exceptional case, to admit that he cannot carry on the Government as he has no majority, and that therefore he cannot accept office unless the King will agree to a dissolution.

But is this equally true of a Prime Minister supported by only a minority in Parliament? Is such a Prime Minister entitled to give advice in regard to dissolution? This question was raised in 1923 when no one political party had a clear majority in the House of Commons and the Liberal Party maintained the balance of power between the Conservative and Labour Parties. Mr. Asquith, the Liberal leader, in a pronouncement at a meeting of the Liberal members of the House of Commons on December 18, 1923, supplied an answer to the questions as to whether Mr. MacDonald as Prime Minister would have the constitutional right to advise the Crown to dissolve Parliament if defeated in the House of Commons after a short tenure of office, and whether the king would be acting in accordance with the spirit of the Constitution in refusing to exercise the prerogative of dissolution when so advised. He said:[9]

The crown is not bound to take the advice of a particular Minister to put its subjects to the tumult and turmoil of a series of general elections so long as it can find other Ministers who are prepared to give it a trial. The notion that a Minister who cannot command a majority in the House of Commons, who is in a minority of 31 per cent—the notion that a Minister in these circumstances is invested with the right to demand a dissolution

[9] Swift MacNeill, "The Prerogative of Dissolution," *The Manchester Guardian Weekly,* December 28, 1923. Cited in Sait and Barrows, *British Politics in Transition* (Yonkers-on-Hudson, N. Y., 1925), pp. 18-22.

is as subversive of constitutional usages as it would . . . be pernicious to the general and paramount interests of the nation at large.

What Mr. Asquith said was a clear indication that he contemplated the possibility of himself assuming office within the term of the existing Parliament, when Mr. MacDonald should have been defeated after being Prime Minister for a few months.[10] Mr. MacDonald however promptly pointed out that if the Labour Government were defeated, the Conservative Party, the largest party in the House of Commons, rather than the Liberal Party, could be asked to form a government.[11] Having expressed his opinion upon the subject, Mr. Asquith did not pursue it further, although his theory of constitutional usage was supported in some quarters and challenged in others. The following year, when the defeat of the Labour Government was certain and a dissolution was imminent, " there were few who doubted that his (Mr. MacDonald's) request would be granted."[12] As a matter of fact, when Mr. MacDonald advised dissolution after he had been defeated, the king very readily assented and Parliament was accordingly dissolved in October, 1924.

The decision of the Prime Minister in rendering advice to the sovereign regarding dissolution, it should be noted, is not based upon his own opinion alone. Professor Ogg observes that " most precedents indicate . . . that such a

[10] *Annual Register,* 1923, English History, p. 142.

[11] Rogers, " The Changing English Constitution," *The North American Review,* vol. 219, pp. 759-768, June, 1924.
Lindsay Rogers further comments on dissolution by a minority party: " If a minority party can dissolve the House of Commons at will, the consequences will be tremendous. The whole plan of parliamentary government in England will be changed. The House of Commons will be able to veto the proposals of a minority of the House only if it is willing thereby to decree its own annihilation."

[12] The London *Times.* October 10, 1924, p. 12.

decision must be reached by the cabinet as a whole and not by the premier alone." [18]   But does it mean that it is the duty of the Cabinet, and not of the Prime Minister, to initiate the idea of dissolution, or that it is the duty of the Prime Minister to advance such an idea and the function of the Cabinet to decide upon it?   Could the Prime Minister advise a dissolution without any knowledge or previous consent on the part of his colleagues in the Cabinet, or is at least the sanction or endorsement of the idea of dissolution by the Cabinet necessary before a dissolution is advised? And finally is the previous consent of the whole Cabinet or that of just a few important members thereof sufficient to empower the Prime Minister to advise a dissolution?   These questions can best be answered by a factual analysis of the much-discussed cases of dissolution and reference to the phenomena common to nearly all of them.

In 1868 Disraeli, after his defeat in the House of Commons on Gladstone's Resolution for the disestablishment of the Irish Church, went to Queen Victoria, without first consulting his colleagues in the Cabinet, to tender the advice that Parliament be dissolved with resignation as an alternative.   " This somewhat high-handed departure from precedent was naturally resented " by his colleagues.   The next day, however, the Cabinet endorsed, though with some hesitation, the course which Disraeli had pursued.[14]   But it should be made clear that ten days before he gave his advice to the Queen, a Cabinet had been called together by him to discuss the course the government should take in case of defeat, and the course decided upon by the Cabinet was exactly the one that he did take, that is, a policy of dissolution in preference to resignation, although it might be true

---

[18] Ogg, *English Government and Politics*, p. 151, fn. 14.

[14] Monypenny and Buckle, *Life of Disraeli* (London, 1910-1920), vol. v, pp. 33-34.

that " Disraeli avoided a preliminary Cabinet (after the defeat) because he had good reason to fear that his colleagues would weaken in their resolution now that the moment for action had arrived, but might be trusted to accept a *fait accompli.*" [15]

In 1874 dissolution was advised by Mr. Gladstone without any knowledge or previous consent of his Cabinet. His intention had, however, been made known to Lord Granville, Lord Cardwell, Bright and Wolverton all of whom, except the last mentioned, were then in the Cabinet,[16] and Lord Granville, Bright and Wolverton, as recorded by Mr. Gladstone himself, " seemed to approve." Furthermore, after dissolution was advised by Mr. Gladstone (on January 21) and granted by the Queen (on January 22) a Cabinet was summoned by the Prime Minister (on January 23) to endorse the step already taken by him. In that Cabinet, his colleagues were said to have " acceded to it (dissolution) without opposition, or . . . even discussion." [17]

Another delicate situation arose in 1923.[18] Confronted with the serious problem of business stagnation and unem-

[15] *Ibid.*, vol. v, pp. 28, 33-34.

[16] *Annual Register,* 1873, pt. ii, p. 252: Lord Granville, Secretary of State for Foreign Affairs; Lord Cardwell, Secretary of State for War; Bright, Chancellor of the Duchy of Lancaster.

[17] Morley, *Life of Gladstone* (New York, 1903), vol. ii, pp. 483-485. Lord Granville in his letter to Queen Victoria on January 21, 1874, mentioned that Mr. Gladstone had consulted Mr. Goschen, the First Lord of the Admiralty, beside Mr. Cardwell and Lord Granville himself and that the three colleagues of Mr. Gladstone were of the opinion that a dissolution would greatly aid in clearing the situation for both parties and for the Queen. *Letters of Queen Victoria 1862–1885* (New York, 1926-1928), vol. ii, p. 305.

[18] For dissolutions between 1874 and 1923, *cf.* the analysis, made by Mr. Asquith, of the Cabinet deliberations of the dissolutions of 1868, 1874, 1880, 1885, 1886, 1892, 1895, 1900, 1906, 1910 (Jan.) and 1910 (Nov.), in his book, *Fifty Years of British Parliament* (Boston, 1926), vol. ii, pp. 217 218.

ployment, Mr. Baldwin, then Prime Minister, in his speech at Plymouth on October 25, suddenly announced that the only way of fighting the unemployment problem was "by protecting the home market" and that he planned to submit his view to the judgment of the electorate.[19] This speech, together with his later speeches at Swansea and Manchester, inevitably led to a General Election which was nevertheless unexpected.[20] According to the material now available, we find that the Cabinet was not yet agreed upon the issue of dissolution when the Plymouth speech was delivered.[21] But since Mr. Neville Chamberlain, at that time Chancellor of the Exchequer, after having heard the opinion of the Prime Minister made a speech advocating in an even more emphatic way the same remedy for unemployment at the same place and on the same day,[22] it might be taken for granted that the idea of dissolution had been previously conveyed by Mr. Baldwin to those ministers in the "inner circle" of the Cabinet. It should be remarked furthermore that at least two Cabinet meetings, aside from conferences between the Prime Minister and former Conservative ministers, were held to deliberate on the question of dissolution, before dissolution was actually advised.[23]

In 1924, long before Mr. MacDonald, the Prime Minister, made his statement about dissolution to the House of Commons, the fact that a dissolution was imminent was known.

[19] The London *Times*, October 26, 1923, p. 17.

[20] *Annual Register*, 1923, English History, pp. 118-132.

[21] Ogg, *English Government and Politics*, p. 151, fn. 14.

[22] The London *Times*, October 26, 1923, p. 17.

[23] Dissolution was announced in Parliament on November 13, and the two Cabinet meetings were held on November 9 and on November 13 (just before the opening of the Parliament). *Cf.*: The London *Times*, Nov. 9, 1923, p. 12; Nov. 10, 1923, p. 12; and Nov. 13, 1923, p. 12. *The New York Times*, Nov. 14, 1923, p. 2.

Although he had announced it at the meeting of the Parliamentary Labour Party,[24] it is still unknown how many of his colleagues in the Cabinet had expressed their approval of his tentative decision in favor of dissolution. Professor Laski writes: [25]

If, in 1924, there were members of Mr. MacDonald's Cabinet who knew that he had decided upon dissolution after the Campbell case, not every member of his Cabinet was consulted.

However, the Cabinet called together by him on October 6, pending the vote on the Liberal Amendment to the Conservative Vote of Censure, decided that: [26]

If either the Vote of Censure or the Liberal Amendment is carried against them the Prime Minister will advise the King to dissolve Parliament.

After another Cabinet meeting held on the day following the government's defeat on the Liberal Amendment (on October 8),[27] therefore, the Prime Minister advised dissolution, and after having secured the assent of the king announced it in the House of Commons on October 9.

It appears from the evidence just given that dissolution is usually initiated or suggested by the Prime Minister and then submitted by him to the Cabinet for decision before it is recommended to the sovereign. The previous consent of a few Cabinet ministers to a proposal of dissolution, without

[24] The London *Times,* October 10, 1924, p. 12.

[25] Laski, *The Crisis and the Constitution: 1931 and After* (London, 1932), p. 12. In his article, " The Dissolution," *Contemporary Review,* vol. 126, pp. 544-552, Nov., 1924, C. F. G. Masterman writes as follows: " For myself, I must confess that the particular and frantic plunge taken by the Labour Prime Minister, against the advice of the saner minds of the Labour Cabinet, came at the last with some surprise."

[26] The London *Times,* Oct. 7, 1924, p. 14.

[27] *Ibid.,* Oct. 10, 1924, p. 12.

the knowledge or approval of the whole Cabinet, is not ordinarily considered sufficient ground for the Prime Minister to request dissolution from the sovereign. The case of 1874 was, it is true, an exception. But the fact should not be lost sight of that, even in that case, when Mr. Gladstone was advising the Queen to call for dissolution, he was not unmindful of " his duty to bring this subject before his colleagues . . . when they will again assemble "; [28] and as a matter of fact the advice given to the Queen was finally endorsed by the Cabinet the next day after it was accepted by her. We may therefore assume that before dissolution is advised by the Prime Minister, the Cabinet is, as a rule, consulted or at least informed. Disraeli's failure, in 1868, in calling a Cabinet meeting after his government's defeat to renew the discussion of dissolution or to reaffirm the decision arrived at in a Cabinet meeting called together before the defeat in anticipation of the unfavourable result in the House of Commons only resulted in resentment, anger and a threat of resignation on the part of his colleagues in the Cabinet.[29] Moreover, the assertion by Mr. Asquith that the dissolution of Parliament is "always submitted to the Cabinet for ultimate decision"[30] seems to imply that dissolution is one of the matters that concern not only the Prime Minister but the whole Cabinet,[31] and that, by giving its ultimate consent to the proposal of dissolution, the Cabinet assumes, as in other matters, a collective responsibility

---

[28] *Letters of Queen Victoria, 1862-1885*, vol. ii, pp. 303-305.

[29] Monypenny and Buckle, *Life of Disraeli*, vol. v, pp. 33-34.

[30] The Earl of Oxford and Asquith, *Fifty Years of British Parliament*, vol. ii, p. 218.

[31] There are some matters, the change of personnel in the Cabinet for instance, which, though of importance in themselves, are in practice never, or hardly ever, brought before the Cabinet. *Cf. Ibid.*, vol. ii, pp. 217-218.

to Parliament [32] which is one of the cardinal principles of
the English government. Although the conception regarding the question as to who should decide the dissolution of
Parliament has, since the war, undergone considerable modi-
fication,[33] yet in practice the general principle is still adhered
to, no matter how dominant the Prime Minister may be,
since his decision is, after all, only tentative in character and
is usually submitted to the Cabinet for approval.

The general principle that dissolution is usually submitted
to the Cabinet for ultimate decision having been established,
the question now is as to how the Cabinet comes to a decision
and what part the Prime Minister plays in the deliberations.
In general, the relation of the Prime Minister to his colleagues " depends very much upon the character " of the
Prime Minister himself.[34] It is, however, " a mistake to

[32] In criticizing Mr. MacDonald's resort to resignation in 1931 without a previous consultation with his colleagues in the Cabinet, Laski says:
" For the whole essence of the right to resign or to dissolve is not to
permit a Prime Minister to appeal from his colleagues to his opponents;
it is to permit a Cabinet defeated in the House of Commons, or desiring
a refreshment of its authority, to seek a new mandate from the
electorate. No Cabinet in the past would have accepted the operation
of that power by the Prime Minister alone on any other terms. And
from this the inference should surely be drawn that its operation cannot
now safely remain the sole prerogative of the Prime Minister. He must
share its existence at least with the Cabinet. They partake of responsibility for his policy; they are entitled to share with him in making the
strategic decisions upon which the shaping of policy depends. A decision
to resign or to dissolve ought at the least to be a Cabinet decision if
collective responsibility is to be real, and if the party is to be real, and
if the party is to be reasonably safeguarded against the possible errors
of its leader." *The Crisis and the Constitution: 1931 and After*, p. 18.

[33] *Cf.* 110 *H. C. Deb.*, 5 s., 2425. 74 *H. L. Deb.*, 5 s., 5-6. Swift
MacNeill, " The Prime Minister and the Prerogative of Dissolution ",
The Fortnightly Review, vol. 117, pp. 744-753, May, 1922.

[34] Gardiner, *Life of Sir William Harcourt* (London, 1923), vol. ii,
Appendix II.

suppose that even the strongest Prime Minister is always the supreme or ultimate arbiter of decisions in his own Cabinet." [35]   Its primary purpose being to arrive at a unanimous decision about a question under consideration,[36] a Cabinet meeting, should the Prime Minister cherish opinions different from those of his colleagues, usually results either in a surrender by the Prime Minister or in an acquiescence by his colleagues.   This is indeed true of Cabinet deliberations on the dissolution of Parliament.   Thus, there have been cases during a Cabinet discussion in which the Prime Minister's insistence on a dissolution has completely submerged the dissenting opinions of his colleagues.   In 1886 a Cabinet meeting was called on the day following the defeat of the government on the second reading of the Home Rule Bill.   It is said [37] that in that meeting three of the ministers

inclined pretty strongly towards resignation as a better course than dissolution; mainly on the ground that the incoming government would then have to go to the country with a policy of their own.   Mr. Gladstone, however, entirely composed though pallid, at once opened the case with a list of twelve reasons for recommending dissolution, and the reasons were so cogent that his opening of the case was also its closing. . . . His conclusion was accepted without comment.

Again, in 1923, the dominance of Mr. Baldwin, to which some reference has already been made, practically overshadowed the opinions of some of his colleagues in the Cab-

[35] The Earl of Oxford and Asquith, *Fifty Years of British Parliament,* vol. ii, pp. 216-7.

[36] Concerning the recent practice of "agreement to differ," a divergence from the theory of Cabinet solidarity, see: Marriott, "Cabinet Government—Its Future", *The Fortnightly Review,* vol. 137, pp. 311-22, March, 1932.

[37] Morley, *Life of Gladstone,* vol. iii, pp. 341-342.

inet and the final determination for dissolution was arrived at only through their unwilling acquiescence.[38]

Furthermore, while there appears to be no instance where the Prime Minister was able to make his opinion in the matter of dissolution prevail against the united opposition of his colleagues, there is at least one case where he was able to secure his wishes with very little numerical support. In 1895 when the Cabinet met after the Government's defeat on the army estimates,[39]

the only alternatives which they seriously considered were resignation and dissolution. The majority were at first un-

[38] On November 9, 1923, preceding the Cabinet meeting to decide the issue of dissolution, the London *Times* (page 12) reported:

"It cannot be denied that some of his (Mr. Baldwin's) most ardent supporters in the Cabinet favour a December election. But there is also a very strong feeling in the Cabinet against such a course, and the general impression is that at the present moment Ministerial feeling on the subject is very evenly divided."

The difference of opinion thus reported may concern merely the date of dissolution, but the letters of Lord Curzon, then Secretary of State for Foreign Affairs, cited below, touched the important issue itself, viz. whether there should be a General Election at all. Lord Curzon wrote in his letter to Lord Crewe on November 12, three days after the Cabinet meeting:

"We are being involved, as I think, quite unnecessarily and unwisely in a conflict that can only be solved by a General Election. That this can strengthen the Government, I can hardly believe; that it may materially weaken us, is at least probable."

Five days later, in a letter to the same correspondent he said:

"Personally, I deeply regret and deplore what I regard as a premature and unnecessary dissolution. But the Prime Minister is very confident." Earl of Ronaldshay, *Life of Lord Curzon* (New York, 1927), vol. iii, p. 364.

[39] The Earl of Oxford and Asquith, *Fifty Years of British Parliament*, vol. i, pp. 260-262. It may be of some interest to note here that an incident was described in *The Greville Memoirs, 1837-1852* (London, 1885), vol. i, pp. 320-321, in which Lord Melbourne, the Prime Minister, in the Cabinet meeting of September 29, 1840, was said to have fallen asleep while Lord John Russell was about to propose a dissolution of Parliament. Consequently, the question was not settled at that meeting.

questionably in favour of dissolution, which I (Mr. Asquith) have never doubted was strategically the right course. But both Rosebery and Harcourt were strong for resignation, and the Cabinet was so impressed by the unusual—the almost unprecedented—spectacle of their cordial agreement with one another, that it deferred to their combined authority, and Lord Rosebery proceeded to place his and their offices at the disposal of the Queen.

As for the cases of the Prime Minister's yielding to his colleagues in a decision either for or against dissolution, the following instances may be cited. In 1841 when the Melbourne Government was becoming weaker and weaker every day, the question of dissolution was brought up. The Cabinet was divided, and the Prime Minister was strongly opposed to this step. In a Cabinet of fifteen, only three ministers were reported to share the view of the Prime Minister,[40] yet the latter's persistence triumphed. When the Cabinet deliberated on the question again, however, after the government's defeat on the Budget on May 18, all the ministers except Lord Melbourne and Lord Normanby expressed their opinion in favor of dissolution. Nevertheless, Lord Melbourne, who was "still against dissolution," very reluctantly assented and reported to Queen Victoria that under the circumstances he felt he "could not but go with them." [41] A situation similar to that of 1841 existed also in 1892, but in this case it concerned only the date of dissolution since the issue of dissolution itself, already determined through the approaching termination of the legal term of Parliament, did not require discussion. The question for Lord Salisbury, the Prime Minister, to decide in May 1892, was whether the

[40] Normanby, Macaulay and Clarendon. See *The Greville Memoirs, 1837-1852*, vol. ii, pp. 4-5, 7-9.

[41] *Letters of Queen Victoria, 1837-1861* (New York, 1907), vol. i, pp. 353-4.

dissolution should take place in the coming June or in October. Mr. Joseph Chamberlain was the only one among Lord Salisbury's colleagues to favor the later date, and Lord Salisbury, as he reported to Queen Victoria, " on general grounds rather leant to Mr. Chamberlain's view; but, in face of the strong opinion of the others . . . accepted the view that the end of June should be selected." [42]

With regard to those cases in which the Prime Minister gave up the idea of dissolution because of the opposition of his colleagues, it is worthy of note that there were two such instances, both of which concerned Mr. Gladstone, who, as Lord Morley remarked, was hardly ever inclined to surrender, at any crisis in his life, short of absolute compulsion.[43] In September, 1893, when Mr. Gladstone desired to dissolve on Home Rule, he was opposed by his colleagues in the Cabinet, so that he gave up the idea, regarding that opposition as decisive.[44] In January of the next year, when the relation between the two Houses of Parliament became strained because of the mutilation and defeat of the Commons' bills by the House of Lords, Mr. Gladstone, then at Biarritz, again suggested dissolution to his colleagues in London [45] who had already made known to him their views that on account of his disagreement with them on the naval estimates he should resign. The telegram he received was " a hopelessly adverse reply " to his suggestion. Nevertheless, after his return, he revived the proposal of a speedy dissolution, but it proved just as fruitless because of a hostile Cabinet. Gladstone was thus finally, to use Lord Morley's

[42] *Letters of Queen Victoria, 1886–1901,* vol. ii, pp. 118-119.

[43] Morley, *op. cit.,* vol. ii, pp. 206-207.

[44] Swift MacNeill, " The Prime Minister and the Prerogative of Dissolution." (See *supra,* p. 34, fn. 33.)

[45] Morley, *op. cit.,* vol. iii, pp. 504-505.

phrase again, "edged out by the ambition and restlessness of colleagues" and he resigned.[46]

In summarizing, we may thus state that Parliament is dissolved by the sovereign only upon the advice of the Prime Minister and that in general the advice of the Prime Minister is in turn based, not upon his own opinion alone, but upon the decision of the whole Cabinet which is arrived at, in case of difference of opinion between the Prime Minister and his colleagues, either through a surrender by the Prime Minister or by an acquiescence by his colleagues. Let us now inquire as to the part which the sovereign actually plays in regard to dissolution. It has been pointed out that since the emergence of ministerial responsibility the sovereign may exercise the prerogative of dissolution only "on the advice and at the request of his ministers", and "for a dissolution of Parliament effected by the sovereign *proprio motu* without the advice or against the advice of his ministers we must go back to the days before responsible government."[47] But is it true that immediately upon the advice of his ministers the sovereign has no choice but must proclaim a dissolution, or may he still exercise some independent judgment before granting a dissolution? In answering this question, we must recognize at the outset that the prerogative of dissolution is, in Mr. Asquith's words, "not a mere feudal survival, but a part, and . . . a useful part" of the English constitutional system.[48] Determination upon dissolution can not be regarded as final and complete without the

---

[46] Morley, *Recollections* (N. Y., 1917), vol. ii, pp. 3-10. *Cf.* further: Crewe, *Lord Rosebery* (New York, 1931), pp. 356-361. The Earl of Oxford and Asquith, *Memories and Reflections, 1852-1927* (Boston, 1928), vol. i, pp. 167-168.

[47] Anson, *The Law and Custom of the Constitution*, vol. i, pp. 304-306. *Cf. supra*, pp. 16, 23.

[48] See *supra*, p. 27, fn. 9.

sanction of the sovereign.[49] And the exercise by the sovereign of independent judgment on the advice given by his ministers necessarily leads to the question whether the sovereign can refuse a dissolution when advised. To this a reply has been supplied by Lord Aberdeen in an oral statement made on May 15, 1851 : [50]

He (Lord Aberdeen) said that he had never entertained the slightest doubt that if the Minister advised the Queen to dissolve, she would, as a matter of course, do so. The Minister who advised the Dissolution took upon himself the heavy responsibility of doing so, but that the Sovereign was bound to suppose that the person whom she had appointed as a Minister was a gentleman and an honest man, and that he would not advise Her Majesty to take such a step unless he thought that it was for the good of the country. There was no doubt of the power and prerogative of the Sovereign to refuse a Dissolution—it was one of the very few acts which the Queen of England could do without responsible advice at the moment; but even in this case whoever was sent for to succeed, must, with his appointment, assume the responsibility of this act, and be prepared to defend it in Parliament.

He could not remember a single instance in which the undoubted power of the Sovereign had been exercised upon this point, and the advice of the Minister to dissolve Parliament had been rejected . . . and that the result of such refusal would be that the Queen would take upon herself the act of dismissing Lord Derby from office, instead of his resigning from being unable longer to carry on the Government.

Although, theoretically, the existence of the power and prerogative of the sovereign to refuse a dissolution is unquestionable, no historical instance can be cited to show that such power has been exercised.[51] The only occasion when Queen

---

[49] Todd, *On Parliamentary Government in England*, vol. ii, p. 509.

[50] *Letters of Queen Victoria, 1837–1861*, vol. iii, pp. 363-366.

[51] In 1839 Queen Victoria signified to Sir Robert Peel, when he was

Victoria contemplated a refusal of dissolution was in the
early part of May, 1886 when she anticipated advice of this
measure from Mr. Gladstone in the event of the defeat of
his Home Rule Bill in the House of Commons. When the
advisability of such a step was put before Lord Salisbury,
the latter replied: [52]

If Mr. Gladstone is refused leave to dissolve, the fact will certainly be known. His *entourage* is far from discreet; and they
are very bitter. The consequence must be that those who are
in favour of Home Rule—the Irish, and the more Radical
English—will think and say, that the action of the Queen is
keeping them from Home Rule. A great deal of resentment
will be excited against the Queen; and, if tempestuous times
should follow, the responsibility will be thrown on her. This
is undesirable, to say the least; especially if no object is to be
gained by it. Whether it would diminish her influence seriously
or not it is difficult to determine; but the risk of such a diminution ought not to be lightly incurred. Her influence is one of
the few bonds of cohesion remaining to the community.

As a result, when dissolution was actually advised by Mr.
Gladstone after the government's defeat on the Home Rule
Bill, the sanction was readily granted by the Queen.[58] The
possibility of a refusal of dissolution has often been talked

attempting to form a government after the resignation of Lord Melbourne, that she hoped that he "did not propose to dissolve Parliament,
and that she had great objections to dissolution." But such an expression on the part of the Queen did not imply that she required any engage-
ment from Sir Robert Peel not to advise dissolution in any contingency
that might occur or that she had an invincible objection to dissolution
even in the event of Peel's inability to command a majority in the
House of Commons. *Sir Robert Peel, From His Private Papers*
(London, 1891-1899), vol. ii, pp. 390-91.

[52] *Letters of Queen Victoria, 1886-1901*, vol. i, pp. 128-130. The same
advice was given by Lord Salisbury on May 22, 1886. *Ibid.*, vol. i,
pp. 134-135.

[53] *Ibid.*, vol. i, pp. 144-145.

about, since 1886, and its realization has sometimes been even expected.   To the theoretical discussion by Mr. Asquith in 1923 about the justification for a refusal to grant a dissolution, we have already referred.   On November 16, 1910, when Mr. Asquith, the Prime Minister, and Lord Crewe, Lord Privy Seal, were going to advise a dissolution, Lord Morley, then Lord President of the Privy Council, told Sir A. Fitzroy that the King's position in refusing the request " was a very strong one, and that of the Government . . . very weak." [54]   Nevertheless, the request was complied with by the King, although (in Lord Crew's phrase) " with legitimate reluctance." [55]   In all these cases, viz., those of 1886, 1910 (November) and 1924 [56] dissolution was, it may be interesting to remark, granted by the sovereign despite the fact that since Parliament in each case had been in existence for just a few months,[57] its dissolution was highly objectionable.[58]

Under special circumstances resignation has been tendered as an alternative to dissolution.   Since a grant of dissolution and acceptance of a resignation were both open to the sovereign, by resorting to either course he would not, even at the moment, incur any responsibility.   The sovereign might, in such a case, refuse to grant a dissolution without jeopardizing the position of the Crown, as such a refusal

[54] Fitzroy, *Memoirs* (London, 5th ed.), vol. ii, pp. 422-423.

[55] Marriott, " The Crown and the Crisis," *Fortnightly Review,* vol. 96, pp. 448-492, September, 1911.

[56] The dissolution about which Mr. Asquith expressed his opinion in 1923 was the dissolution which Mr. MacDonald might resort to after he had become Prime Minister and not the dissolution which had just taken place (the dissolution of 1923).

[57] Those three Parliaments which were shortest in duration among the Parliaments in the last hundred years existed only for 164, 281 and 266 days respectively.

[58] Todd, *op. cit.,* vol. ii, p. 507.

would amount merely to an acceptance of resignation. Yet, in 1859 [59] and in 1868 [60] when the government advised dissolution with resignation as an alternative, Queen Victoria, in both cases, granted a dissolution instead of choosing the other course.

Although the power and prerogative of the sovereign to " cause " a dissolution, like his power and prerogative to refuse a dissolution, still exists; it has not in constitutional practice been exercised,[61] with the possible exception of the dissolution of 1834. In that year, seizing the opportunity which the death of Lord Spencer [62] presented for the elevation to the House of Lords of his son, Lord Althorp, the Chancellor of the Exchequer and Leader of the House of Commons, William IV dismissed [63] Lord Melbourne from

[59] 153 *Hansard* (Lords) 3 s., 1289.

[60] Monypenny and Buckle, *Life of Disraeli*, vol. v, pp. 30-32.

[61] Anson, *op. cit.*, vol. i, pp. 308-309.

[62] About the causes of the dismissal, *cf. Lord Melbourne's Papers* (London, 1889), pp. 224-226.

[63] The action of William IV in causing the downfall of the Melbourne Government in 1834 is generally regarded as a dismissal. The word "dismissal" should however be used with some reserve. For, before Lord Melbourne was discharged from office, he told, or, perhaps we should say, advised, the King that ". . . in the new and altered circumstances it is for your Majesty to consider whether it is your pleasure to authorize Viscount Melbourne to make such fresh arrangements as may enable your Majesty's present servants to continue to conduct the affairs of the country, or whether your Majesty deems it advisable to adopt any other course." (*Lord Melbourne's Papers*, pp. 219-221.) If that should be considered as a tender of resignation, the discharge by the King would only amount to its acceptance. [*Cf.* Maxwell, *Life of Wellington* (London, 1899), vol. ii, pp. 301-302.] Basing his opinion upon this letter from Melbourne to William IV, J. H. Morgan even went so far as to say that "King William the Fourth's dismissal of Melbourne in 1834 is now universally recognized . . . as a resignation rather than a dismissal." ("The King and His Prerogative," *The Nineteenth Century and After*, vol. 70, pp. 215-225, August, 1911.) Moreover, the fact that Lord Melbourne consented to be the bearer of a summons to the Duke of Wellington for the formation of a government to succeed himself

the office on the ground that the ministers " are not strong enough in the Commons to carry on the business of the country." [64]   In taking this action he was not unaware of the fact that the dismissal of the Melbourne Government, which was supported by a majority in the House of Commons, would precipitate a dissolution of Parliament. In fact, he resorted to dismissal of the ministry, because he believed that the general election which was to follow would sweep away the majority which supported the Melbourne ministry.[65]   As Baron Stockmar remarked, " if he delayed coming to a decision the opportunity of dissolving the Parliament during its prorogation . . . would be lost." [66]   That is the reason why the King after having received Lord Melbourne's letter telling him the courses from which he might choose in order to meet the new and altered situation caused by the removal of Lord Althorp, could very readily make his mind up to inform Lord Melbourne that: [67]

he conceives that the general weight and consideration of the present Government is so much diminished in the House of

(*Lord Melbourne's Papers*, p. 223), might also be taken to imply previous consent on the part of Lord Melbourne to the King's action in relieving him of office.

On the other hand, it should also be borne in mind that Lord Melbourne was still aiming at a reorganization of the Cabinet, instead of its resignation, when the King told him that ". . . His Majesty . . . does not think it would be acting *fairly* or honorably by his lordship to call upon the Viscount for the continuance of his service in a position of which the tenure appears to the King to be so precarious." (*Ibid.*, pp. 222-3.)   In fact, it was only after the King's written communication had been submitted to his colleagues that Lord Melbourne was directed by them formally to tender their resignation. *Ibid.*, pp. 226-7.

[64] *Memoirs of Baron Stockmar* (London, 1873), vol. i, p. 309.

[65] Torrens, *Memoirs of Viscount Melbourne* (London, 1878), vol. ii, p. 39.

[66] *Memoirs of Baron Stockmar*, vol. i, pp. 334-345.

[67] *Lord Melbourne's Papers*, pp. 222-223.

Commons, and in the country at large, as to render it impossible that they should continue to conduct the public affairs in the Commons. . . .

Subsequent to the episode of 1834, there arose a great many occasions on which the sovereign attempted either to suggest or to press for a dissolution. It may be worth while to analyze briefly in each case how far the sovereign did go in that direction and how much he accomplished.

In 1852, before the Russell Government resigned on account of defeat on the Militia Bill in the House of Commons, Queen Victoria offered it the alternative of a dissolution of Parliament. But the Cabinet was unanimous in the opinion that it would not be advisable to make use of the Queen's permission to advise a dissolution and that there was no other course to pursue but that of resignation.[68]

In 1857, on the day when the Palmerston Government was defeated in the House of Commons on Cobden's Resolution on the China War, Queen Victoria informed the Prime Minister through Prince Albert that she felt[69]

herself physically quite unable to go through the anxiety of a Ministerial Crisis and the fruitless attempt to form a new Government out of the heterogeneous elements out of which the present opposition is composed, should the Government feel it necessary to offer their resignation, and would on that account *prefer any other alternative.* . . .

How much influence the preference for dissolution on the part of the Queen had on the Cabinet decision for an appeal to the country, it is well-nigh impossible to estimate. It is, however, certain that Lord Palmerston, who was then tremendously popular in the country and who has been challenged by Disraeli in the House of Commons on the question

---

[68] *Letters of Queen Victoria, 1837–1861,* vol. ii, pp. 445-446.
[69] *Ibid.,* vol. iii, p. 290.

of dissolution,[70] would not resort to an appeal to the country merely because of the preference of the Crown.

On April 25, 1866, on notification from Lord John Russell that the Cabinet would deliberate upon the choice between resignation and dissolution in case of the Government's defeat in the House of Commons on the Reform Bill, Queen Victoria implicitly manifested her preference for dissolution by offering to the Cabinet the following " considerations," [71] despite the short tenure the Parliament had had: [72]

First: The country is said not to be anxious for a change of Government.

Secondly: Is there any chance, if there should be one, of its being *able* to stand?

Thirdly: Ought not the Country to be asked to pronounce its opinion on the subject of Reform?

Fourthly: If a Conservative Government were to come in, they would probably also ask for a dissolution, and considering that this Parliament was returned to support Lord Palmerston, it might be difficult to refuse it, consequently the danger of agitation would not be avoided.

On June 18 when the Government was defeated the Cabinet, not adhering to the Queen's advice, preferred resignation, and accordingly the Russell Government went out of existence on June 26, 1866.

The Disraeli Government being confronted, in 1868, with Mr. Gladstone's Resolutions on disestablishment of the Irish Church, determined that in order to meet Mr. Gladstone's motion to go into Committee on his Resolutions Stanley should move a temporizing amendment which, " while admitting that considerable modifications in Irish Church temporalities might be expedient," would at the same time declare

---

[70] Monypenny and Buckle, *Life of Disraeli*, vol. iv, pp. 73-74.

[71] *Letters of Queen Victoria, 1862–1885*, vol. i, p. 320.

[72] The Parliament began its first Session on April 1, 1857.

that "the decision of the question should be left to a new Parliament." That amendment was defeated by sixty votes, and the motion to go into Committee was carried by fifty-six. At that juncture, when resignation or dissolution was inevitable if the government should be defeated when the Resolutions were moved in detail, Queen Victoria expressed herself strongly against resignation in a private talk with Lord Derby on April 3, and entertained at Windsor during the Easter recess not only Disraeli, the Prime Minister who agreed with her, but also Hardy and Cairnes, Cabinet ministers who held different opinions. She impressed her view very strongly upon them all. Before the recess was concluded, she had another conference with Disraeli. Through all these audiences the Queen who, as she told Disraeli on April 22, 1868, always believed that the question of disestablishment of the Irish Church could not " be settled without an appeal to the country " was able to exert some influence in persuading the Cabinet to sanction, in anticipation of the forthcoming debate on the first and main resolution brought up by Gladstone after the resumption of Parliament, a policy of dissolution in preference to resignation. Acting in accordance with this policy Disraeli, after the Government's defeat, tendered his advice for dissolution with resignation as an alternative.[73]

The Gladstone Government was defeated on July 8, 1884 by a majority of 59 in the House of Lords on the second reading of the Franchise Bill. On the Prime Minister's advice for a prorogation instead of a dissolution of Parliament, Queen Victoria said in her letter of July 10 that, while not withholding her assent to his proposal for an Autumn Session in order to reconsider the defeated bill, she considered that:

[73] Monypenny and Buckle, *op. cit.*, vol. v, pp. 19 *et seq.*

it would have been a more fair and judicious course to have dissolved Parliament so as to have obtained the opinion of the country on the questions raised in the House of Lords.

This would have prevented any agitation which the Queen fears may be raised by the postponement of the measure. The opinion of the people constitutionally given at the polling booths is far more valuable than the excitement forced on by the noisy demagogues.

To this the government replied that the views of the country might be learned from the meetings and speeches during the recess and that it would introduce a Redistribution Bill the following session and would make every effort to secure its passage. But such a reply from the government failed to stop the Queen from reminding Mr. Gladstone, on July 13, of " the importance of maintaining the constitutional balance and of opposing the demands of those who desire to wreck existing institutions." This warning on the part of the sovereign led to a very important pronouncement from Mr. Gladstone in his letter to the Queen on July 14:

at no period of our history, known to him, has the House of Commons been dissolved at the call of the House of Lords, given through an adverse vote; . . . in his opinion the establishment of such a principle would place the House of Commons in a position of inferiority, as a Legislative Chamber, to the House of Lords, and . . . the attempt to establish it would certainly end in organic changes, detrimental to the dignity and authority of the House of Lords.

After that, the Queen evidently did not pursue further her effort to secure a dissolution, especially since it had been made known to her that the Conservative Opposition did not wish her to force it.[74]

In July, 1893, contemplating the possibility that, should

[74] *Letters of Queen Victoria, 1862–1885*, vol. iii, pp. 511-513, 515-18, 521.

the Home Rule Bill be defeated in the House of Lords, Mr. Gladstone might not resign, but might re-introduce the bill, Queen Victoria thought that she " ought to insist on a Dissolution on the Home Rule Bill." She consulted the Duke of Argyll and through him also secured personal advice from Lord Salisbury, the Duke of Devonshire and Mr. Chamberlain. The first three agreed that the Queen undoubtedly had the right to do so, but the Duke of Argyll " was not sure of the prudence of doing so " while Lord Salisbury and the Duke of Devonshire thought that " the time had not yet come for such a step." Only Mr. Chamberlain was anxious for a dissolution and even suggested it.[75] The matter however was dropped with the defeat of the Home Rule Bill in the House of Lords, since after such defeat the bill was not re-introduced.

Queen Victoria, in 1894, on the notification by Lord Rosebery, the Prime Minister, that he would shortly announce his policy regarding the reform of the House of Lords, wrote to the Prince of Wales telling him [76]

I am inclined to favour a dissolution sooner than consent to any step which implies tampering with the Constitution, but I must first ascertain what the chances of the Unionists are, so don't mention this.

Furthermore, she asked the Prince to convey to Lord Rosebery his, rather than her, feeling on the policy regarding the House of Lords. The reply from the Prince was that Lord Rosebery " cannot give an opinion whether dissolution just now would be advisable." [77] A few days later (on October 30) the Queen wrote to Lord Rosebery informing him that [78]

---

[75] *Letters of Queen Victoria, 1886–1901*, vol. ii, pp. 278–279, 282.

[76] *Ibid.*, vol. ii, p. 431.

[77] *Ibid.*, vol. ii, pp. 431-432.

[78] *Ibid.*, vol. ii, pp. 437-438.

the Queen thinks that the sense of the country should be taken
before people's passions are aroused by agitation and misrep-
resentation of the House of Lords.

Lord Rosebery in his reply on the next day, however, " entirely ignored that part of (the) Queen's letter saying she
thought there should be dissolution." [79]   The Queen then
consulted with Sir Henry James, the Duke of Devonshire,
the Duke of Argyll, the Marquis of Salisbury, Mr. Balfour
and Mr. Chamberlain.   Sir Henry James's view, later concurred in by the Duke of Devonshire, the Duke of Argyll
and the Marquis of Salisbury,[80] was that the time had not
come for the Queen to insist upon a dissolution of Parliament.   A part of Sir Henry James's long Memorandum of
November 5, 1894 may be quoted in this connection: [81]

If the Prime Minister were to acquiesce in the view that a
Dissolution should now take place, he would necessarily have to
explain his departure from the course he and his colleagues
have announced to be their intention to take.   It would thus
become known that the Dissolution was the result of her
Majesty's personal action.   In such event, in all probability all
other questions, including the desirability of limiting the power
of the House of Lords, would be put aside, and the elections
would turn solely upon considerations affecting the treatment
of the Ministry.   But, if Lord Rosebery were to refuse to
acquiesce in a Dissolution, he would constitutionally be within
his right in doing so.   Of course, the Ministry would under
such circumstances resign and the Queen would have to seek
new advisers.   Dissolution would then become a necessity, but
no expression of opinion upon the wisdom of limiting the power
of the House of Lords would then be directly obtained.

If Lord Rosebery be allowed to carry out the policy he has

[79] *Ibid.*, vol. ii, pp. 439-442.
[80] *Ibid.*, vol. ii, pp. 445-449.
[81] *Ibid.*, vol. ii, pp. 442-444.

announced, he can effect no fundamental changes in the constitution without the consent of the Crown and the House of Lords. No measure disapproved of by the House of Lords can be carried without the creation of some 500 Peers. If such a proposition were submitted to her Majesty, resort to a Dissolution would probably meet with public approval. If, too, Ministers were to present to Parliament a Bill of a very revolutionary or destructive character, her Majesty might well determine that the time had arrived for affording the nation an opportunity of approving or condemning the policy of her Government.

But I most humbly suggest that as yet nothing has been accomplished or definitely proposed upon which the opinion of the nation can with advantage be taken.

Queen Victoria's action in pressing for a dissolution on the issue of the House of Lords was evidently delayed on account of the strong resistance thus shown by the opposition leaders, and was finally dropped because of the assurance from Lord Rosebery that: [82]

there really was no danger, and that there would be nothing more than a resolution, which would result in nothing. There would be a dissolution, in which the Government would most likely be beaten, and . . . the result would be that the House of Lords would be reformed by the Conservative Party.

From the foregoing passages the inference may be drawn that the answer to the question as to whether the sovereign would suggest and press for a dissolution and as to how far he would go in that direction depends very largely upon who the sovereign was, how important the issue involved was, what party was in power and the relations between the sovereign and the ministers. When the throne was occupied by William IV, a dissolution was actually precipitated by the action of the wearer of the Crown in dismissing the min-

[82] *Ibid.*, vol. ii, pp. 455-456.

istry in 1834. Although this precedent was not followed by any of his successors, yet Queen Victoria more than once attempted to insist on a dissolution of Parliament. In 1868 she exerted some influence in forcing dissolution on the disestablishment of the Irish Church, and would have insisted on another dissolution in 1893 if Mr. Gladstone had re-introduced the Home Rule Bill after its defeat in the House of Lords. The same might have been done by George V during the fight over Home Rule in 1914 had he, as some Conservatives expected him to do, forced a decision of the electorate on the question of whether the Liberal Party, in insisting on the inclusion of Ulster, had the support of public opinion. But "those wanting a dissolution through the action of the King . . . were crying in a wilderness and their voices were not heard." [88] While Queen Victoria asked for a dissolution in 1893 on the defeat of the Franchise Bill by the House of Lords and in 1894 on the issue of the reform of the House of Lords, Edward VII, on the defeat of the budget by the House of Lords in 1909, and George V, on the issue of reform of the House of Lords in 1910, played, as is generally known, an inactive and acquiescent part, the dissolution of January, 1910 being granted by the former (Edward VII) only at the request of his impatient Prime Minister [84] and that of November, 1910, by the latter (George V) " with legitimate reluctance."

The gravity of the issue involved, like the character of the sovereign, may serve as the cause of insistence by the Crown on a dissolution. In 1852, 1857, and 1866 Queen Victoria expressed her preference for dissolution; but since the issues involved were not of far-reaching social and constitutional significance, she did not go beyond an expression

---

[83] Rogers, "The Changing English Constitution," see *supra*, p. 28, fn. 11.

[84] Lee, *King Edward VII* (London, 1925-1927), vol. ii, pp. 668-669.

of preference and she showed little concern whether her preference had any effect on the decision by the ministry. However, in the case of issues which touched upon the very foundation of the Constitution or the social structure, she would strongly insist on having a mandate on the question involved and would not give in until she was convinced, as in 1884 and 1894, that further insistence would result in a constitutional crisis and a diminution of the prestige of the Crown while the sovereign would incur a great responsibility.

Finally, the tendency of a sovereign to insist on dissolution depends upon the party in power and the relations between the sovereign and the ministers. Among the cases cited above that of 1868 was the only occasion on which a sovereign insisted on a dissolution when the Tories were in office. William IV, in 1834, would have preferred a reorganization of the ministry to its dismissal and the dissolution which was thereby necessitated, had he not strong objection to some of his ministers, especially Lord John Russell and Lord Brougham, remaining in his Cabinet.[85] Queen Victoria's action in 1884 and 1893 might be attributed in part to her " distrust and dislike " of Mr. Gladstone [86] and her reliance upon the leading Conservatives in the Opposition [87] for counsel regarding dissolution. Her insistence on a dissolution on the question of the reform of the House of Lords in October, 1894, was given up only on the personal assurance of Lord Rosebery, who half a year before had

[85] Cf. *Memoirs of Baron Stockmar*, vol. i, pp. 324-334. *Sir Robert Peel, From His Private Papers*, vol. ii, pp. 264-265.

[86] Strachey, *Queen Victoria* (N. Y., 1931), pp. 327-328.

[87] Concerning the right of the sovereign to consult counsellors, other than the ministers for the moment responsible, cf. Marriott, " The Crown and the Crisis," *The Fortnightly Review*, vol. 136, pp. 579-589, Nov., 1931. Marriott, " The ' Mystery ' of the Monarchy," *The Fortnightly Review*, vol. 134, pp. 770-783, Dec., 1930.

become Prime Minister,[88] that no danger was involved in the course pursued by the government.

As to the measure of success attained by various sovereigns in " causing" a dissolution, it may be held to be true that since 1834 no Parliament has been dissolved merely because of the preference or insistence of the Crown. The dissolution of 1857 was resorted to because of other reasons, as well as the Queen's physical inability to go through the anxiety of a ministerial change,[89] and when Queen Victoria in 1868 tried to impress her view upon the Cabinet ministers, Mr. Disraeli, the Prime Minister, and Lord Derby were likewise in favor of dissolution in the event of the government's defeat on the disestablishment of the Irish Church, although her influence in persuading other ministers to arrive at a decision for dissolution in preference to resignation should not be overlooked.[90]

Thus far we have discussed the parts played by the sovereign, the Prime Minister and the Cabinet in regard to the exercise of the prerogative of dissolution. Now, let us endeavour to determine how far such a prerogative is limited by statute and the part played by the two Houses of Parliament. Before proceeding with this topic, however, we should discuss parenthetically a very interesting governmental practice, generally falling under the name " the threat of dissolution," which involves not only the ministry and the sovereign but the Parliament as well.

In May 1858, Lord Derby, confronted with a vote of censure in both Houses of Parliament on a Despatch con-

[88] *Letters of Queen Victoria, 1886–1901,* vol. ii, pp. 455-456: He (Lord Rosebery) could not well say this to his colleagues, nor did he wish to write it, but he wanted me to know it, begging me not to mention it to anyone.

[89] *Cf.* 144 *Hansard* (Commons) 3 s., 1894-1897.

[90] Monypenny and Buckle, *Life of Disraeli,* vol. v, pp. 26-28.

demning the conduct of the Governor General of India,[91] asked, in an audience with Queen Victoria, " her permission to be allowed to announce that, in the event of an adverse majority, he had Her Majesty's sanction to a Dissolution of Parliament." The Queen at once refused to grant her sanction for such an announcement on the ground that " it would be a very unconstitutional threat for him to hold over the head of the Parliament, with her authority, by way of biasing their decision." [92] On the day after this refusal Lord Derby, in another audience with the Queen, informed her that:

He expects to be beaten by from 15 to 35 votes . . . but thinks still that he could be saved if it were known that the Queen had not refused a Dissolution. . . . He begged again to be empowered to contradict the assertion.

With this request the Queen did not comply at first, but finally she " allowed him to know that a dissolution would not be refused to him, and trusted that her honour would be safe in his hands as to the use he made of that knowledge." [93] Upon that occasion Lord Aberdeen remarked that the Government, in his opinion, had a perfect right to threaten a dissolution, but " they would have been quite wrong in joining the Queen's name with it." [94] So the general theory in regard to the threat of dissolution, as Disraeli said in 1868, is that the sovereign's " sanction to the course recommended " by his ministers " should not be accorded *contingently,* but . . . it should be . . . (if he so pleases) accorded *after* the event of the division." [95]

[91] 150 *Hansard* (Commons) 3 s., 674-761. 150 *Hansard* (Lords), 3 s., 579-673.

[92] *Letters of Queen Victoria, 1837–1861,* vol. iii, pp. 363-366.

[93] *Ibid.,* vol. iii, pp. 367-368.

[94] *Ibid.,* vol. iii, p. 364.

[95] *Letters of Queen Victoria, 1862–1885,* vol. i, pp. 523-526.

So far as the ministry is concerned, the theory seems to be that it is also unconstitutional for it to pledge itself to advise the sovereign to dissolve Parliament before an emergency arises. On March 19, 1852, Lord John Russell in the House of Commons, referring to a precedent in 1841, asked Mr. Disraeli, the Chancellor of the Exchequer, whether the government was prepared to advise the Crown to dissolve. In reply, Mr. Disraeli immediately pointed out that the situation then existing differed from that of 1841 in that the government still stood uncondemned while the government of 1841 had already been defeated. Consequently, while showing no hesitation in revealing the government's intention to advise the sovereign to dissolve as soon as the " necessary measures " should have been passed, he emphatically alleged that Lord John Russell's question was unprecedented, and that it would be unconstitutional for the government to give such a pledge. He said:[96]

I think it is highly unconstitutional and most impolitic that Her Majesty's Government should pledge themselves to advise Her Majesty to dissolve Parliament at a stated and specific period. The noble Lord must feel that circumstances might suddenly arise which would render the fulfillment of such a pledge not only injurious, but perhaps even impracticable.

On the other hand, the ministry may, if it so chooses, and provided the name of the sovereign be not introduced, threaten a dissolution, merely by hinting that if certain things are done, or not done, there will be a General Election. Through this means, as Sidney Low says, " the Ministry can often subdue rebellion in its own ranks, and to a certain extent keep its antagonists from going to extremities." Naturally, however, such a threat, although cogent in the earlier period of the life of a Parliament, is not effective

[96] 119 *Hansard* (Commons) 3 s., 1299-1302.

toward the end, when the Members will grow callous, know-
ing that the Parliament is near its legal termination and that
in any case the dissolution cannot be long deferred.[97]

We shall now turn to consider the statutory limitation
imposed on the prerogative of dissolution. This was formerly two-fold. From 1696 [98] to 1867,[99] Parliament, according to the stipulation of law, was required to be dissolved

[97] Low, *The Governance of England* (London, 1904), pp. 107-111.
Sidney Low on pp. 109-111 of the book mentioned gives the following
instance of a threat of dissolution:

" On June 25, 1904, when the Unionists were much demoralized, and
very slack in their attendances, Mr. Balfour was asked whether he
would not ' withdraw all seriously contentious measures and wind up the
business of the Session in order to submit the policy of Ministers to
the judgment of the country.' The Prime Minister issued the following
written reply to this question: ' I do not propose to take the course
suggesed by the hon. member, unless the Government incur such a
defeat as proves that they have lost the confidence of the House of
Commons; or unless they fail to secure that day-to-day support which
is necessary in order effectively to carry on Parliamentary business. In
either of these events they would, of course, ask relief from responsibilities which they are not sustaining for their own comfort or satisfaction.'

" One of Mr. Balfour's supporters in the press dotted the ' i's ' the
next day, with the following candid observations: ' Members should bear
in mind that *elections are expensive* and, if unsuccessful, extremely
mortifying things. Counter attractions during the next few weeks may
perhaps tempt members to risk the Government's defeat on a snap
division. But we would remind those gentlemen that their carelessness,
if continued, *will probably involve the substitution of an Election
Expenses Bill for the rent of a grouse moor,* besides a possible defeat
at the polls, and the installation once again of Sir Henry Campbell-
Bannerman and his Little Englander Brigade in Downing Street. We
are convinced that Mr. Balfour has uttered no idle threat, and we
sincerely hope, for the good of the country, that lazy members will take
his warning seriously to heart'."

[98] 7 & 8 Will. III, c. 15. The application of this law was explicitly
extended to Scotland in 1707 by 6 Anne, c. 7, and implicitly extended to
Ireland in 1808 by 40 Geo. III, c. 67.

[99] The Representation of the People Act, 1867, 30 & 31 Vict., c. 102.
The Act explicitly prescribed that it " shall not apply to Scotland or
Ireland," but when the question whether fresh elections in Scotland and

in case of the demise of the Crown, although dissolution was not to take place immediately upon the death of the sovereign. But since the later date Parliament has not been dissolved on account of the demise of the Crown. The other limitation concerns the maximum duration of a Parliament. From 1716 to 1911 a Parliament could exist for as long a period as seven years,[100] but in 1911 the term was reduced to five years.[101] As a result, the only existing statutory limitation to the prerogative of dissolution is that at most a Parliament can exist for only five years and must be dissolved when it has been in existence for that length of time, unless a contrary stipulation should be prescribed by law. The only occasions since 1716 when the duration of Parliament was extended were during the World War. The Parliament of 1911 was then extended five times altogether, making its term cover a period of three more years.[102]

Having considered the statutory limitation to the prerogative of dissolution, we now come to the question of whether

Ireland would be necessary in case of the demise of the Crown was referred to the Law Officers of the Crown, it was advised that the intent of the Act was obvious and that there would be no necessity for fresh elections. *Cf.* Lucy, *The Balfourian Parliament, 1900–1905* (London, 1906), p. 20.

[100] The Septennial Act, 1716, 1 Geo. 1, Stat. 2, c. 38.

[101] The Parliament Act, 1911, 1 & 2 Geo. V, c. 13.

[102] 27th Jan., 1916, 5 & 6 Geo. V, c. 100.
   23rd Aug., 1916, 6 & 7 Geo. V, c. 44.
   26th Apr., 1917, 7 & 8 Geo. V, c. 13.
   29th Nov., 1917, 7 & 8 Geo. V, c. 50.
   30th July, 1918, 8 & 9 Geo. V, c. 22.

The postponement of dissolution was, as a matter of fact, determined by the Cabinet and given statutory effect through arrangement of the Cabinet with the Opposition. (The Earl of Oxford and Asquith, *Memories and Reflections, 1852–1927,* vol. ii, pp. 27-8.) Hence the only limitation to the prerogative could, if the circumstances justified, be removed at least for a limited time by the Cabinet if it could secure the consent of the Opposition.

the two Houses of Parliament can exert some measure of control over the exercise of such a prerogative. In general, either House has the undoubted right to address the Crown, praying that Parliament may or may not be dissolved, or to express an opinion in regard to the circumstances under which this prerogative has been exercised.[103] Since the sovereign has become more and more impotent in refusing or in pressing for dissolution, both Houses of Parliament as well as the people who, before the establishment of the idea of Cabinet responsibility, also used to address the Crown about dissolution, no longer find it convenient to address the Crown in order to force or to prevent a dissolution.[104] Thus, in August, 1893, when a group of leading Unionists brought up for discussion the question whether, after the rejection of the Home Rule Bill in the House of Lords, the Queen should be approached either by way of petition, signed on a large scale, or by address from the House of Lords, praying her to exercise her prerogative of dissolution, Lord Salisbury, then in opposition, objected to such a step mainly on the following grounds : [105]

A Dissolution by the Queen, against the advice of her Ministers would, of course, involve their resignation. Their party could hardly help going to the country as the opponents of the royal authority; or at least, as the severe critics of the mode in which it had been exerted. No one can foresee what the upshot of

[103] 153 *Hansard* (Commons) 3 s., 1415-1417. May, *The Constitutional History of England* (Boston, 1862), vol. i, p. 432. Todd, *On Parliamentary Government in England*, vol. ii, p. 510.

[104] For the instances in which the House of Lords and the House of Commons and the people addressed or attempted to address the Crown in regard to dissolution before 1832, see May, *op. cit.*, vol. i, pp. 70-71, 380-382, 431-433. *The Greville Memoirs, A Journal of the Reigns of King George IV and King William IV* (London, 1875), vol. ii, pp. 134-137.

[105] *Letters of Queen Victoria, 1886-1901*, vol. ii, pp. 297-299.

such a state of things would be. It might be good or it might be bad! But there must be *some* hazard that in the end, such a step would injure the authority of the Queen.

The two Houses have, therefore, preferred other courses of action in order to make their influence felt. The House of Commons, or rather chiefly the official Opposition in the House of Commons, would attempt as it did in 1905 and 1909, to force a dissolution through an Amendment to the Address in reply to the Speech from the Throne, and would, as it attempted to do in 1833, 1874 and 1923, censure the government on a dissolution which had just been announced or which had already taken place. But it should be made clear that even if the House had succeeded in 1905 and in 1909, in carrying the Amendment to the Address expressing the desire for an appeal to the country on the fiscal question [106] and on the question " which of the two Houses of Parliament enjoys the confidence of a majority of the electors," [107] the dissolution would not thereby have been determined. The crucial point is that the power of dissolution is a royal pre-

[106] Mr. Asquith's Amendment to the Address reads as follows:

" At the end of the question, to add the words, ' And we humbly represent to your Majesty that, the various aspects of the fiscal question having now been fully discussed in the country for nearly two years, the time has come for submitting the issue to the people without further delay'."

This Amendment was defeated by a vote of 311 to 248 in the House or Commons on February 16, 1905. 141 *Hansard* (Commons) 4 s., 329-428.

[107] Mr. F. E. Smith's Amendment to the Amendment to the Address reads as follows:

" To leave out from ' imperative' to end, and insert ' in the interests of stable Government to decide forthwith by an appeal to the constituencies which of the two Houses of Parliament enjoys the confidence of a majoriy of the electors'."

This Amendment to the Amendment was defeated on February 22, 1909 by a vote of 282 to 71, while the Amendment itself was defeated by a vote of 225 to 47. 1 *H. C. Deb.*, 5 s., 442-554.

rogative and that it is only as ministers of the Crown that
the Prime Minister and his colleagues can give advice to
the sovereign about dissolution. By giving advice, they
incur responsibility to the House of Commons on the question
of dissolution. In order to enforce that responsibility, the
House of Commons may, if it is deemed necessary, withdraw
its confidence by a Vote of Censure on the government for
advice for dissolution or the omission of such an act. The
ministry, as a result of the withdrawal of confidence, may
resort either to a resignation or to a dissolution. According
to constitutional practice, an Amendment to the Address is
regarded as equivalent to a Vote of Censure.[108] Hence, even
if the Amendment to the Address expressing a desire for a
dissolution (to which the ministry ought, as the House
thinks, to have resorted but for which it has not yet advised)
should pass, the ministry may not decide upon a dissolution
for it may choose resignation as an alternative. And in
case dissolution is preferred, such a dissolution should properly be considered as a result of the exercise of the royal
prerogative rather than as the execution of the resolution of
the House of Commons, as expressed in the Amendment to
the Address, calling for an appeal to the country. For the

[108] Confronted with Mr. Asquith's Amendment to the Address, Mr.
Austen Chamberlain, the Chancellor of the Exchequer, said on behalf
of the government on February 15, 1905, that the question brought
before the House was "a clear question of confidence" in the government and that the government is "as ready and anxious as he to have
the verdict of the House on that question", although scarcely had the
word "House" been spoken then the opposition shouted "The Country".
141 *Hansard* (Commons) 4 s., 191.

Upon the Amendment to the Address (to which Mr. F. E. Smith
further proposed his Amendment) being proposed by A. A. W. H.
Ponsonby on February 22, 1909, Mr. Asquith, the Prime Minister, said:

"According to well-settled constitutional practice an Amendment to
the Address is regarded as equivalent to a Vote of Censure upon the
Government. . ." 1 *H. C. Deb.*, 5 s., 456.

House of Commons is not constitutionally entitled to vote for its own dissolution.

Resignation is the natural result of the passage of a Vote of Censure on the government for advice for a dissolution, advice which has already been rendered and which has subsequently caused a General Election, since, the country having just been appealed to, another dissolution will not be available.   This was precisely the situation in 1835 regarding the resignation of the Peel Government which was caused by the defeat on the Vote of Censure on dissolution [109] together with defeats on other matters.[110]   The Vote of Censure, moved on April 24, 1874 by Mr. Smollett on his own responsibility and "not . . . in accord with any party in the House," was directed to the former Prime Minister, Mr. Gladstone, who had, on account of the result of his appeal to the electorate, already relinquished the office in favor of Mr. Disraeli.   In addition to censure of Mr. Gladstone's

[109] The Amendment to the Address proposed by Lord Morpeth was as follows:

"After the words, 'To promote the concord and happiness of my subjects,' in the last paragraph but two (of the Address), these words be inserted: '. . . To represent to his Majesty, that his Majesty's faithful Commons beg leave submissively to add, that they can not but lament that the progress of these (the Policy to 'place, without delay, our Municipal Corporations under vigilant popular control, remove all those unfounded grievances of the Protestant Dissenters, and correct those abuses in the Church which impair its efficiency in England, disturb society in Ireland, and lower the character of the establishment in both countries') and other Reforms, has been interrupted and endangered by the unnecessary dissolution of a Parliament earnestly intent upon the vigorous prosecution of measures to which the wishes of the people were most anxiously and justly directed'."

This Amendment was passed in the House of Commons on February 26, 1835, by a vote of 309 to 302. 26 *Hansard* (Commons) 3 s., 172-173, 325-415.

About the Vote of Censure on dissolution before 1832, cf. Todd, *On Parliamentary Government in England,* vol. i, pp. 145, 160.

[110] See *infra,* p. 154, fn. 93.

action, it was designed to prevent a repetition of a surprise dissolution.[111] But so far as Mr. Gladstone's action was concerned, this vote, which failed of passage,[112] would have had only a moral effect, since Mr. Gladstone had already been in the Opposition. The Vote of Censure on dissolution announced on November 13, 1923 was moved, in the House of Commons which was to be dissolved, by Mr. MacDonald, the Leader of the Opposition, two days after the announcement and defeated by a vote of 285 to 190.[113] It is evident that that vote, had it been passed, would not have produced

[111] Mr. Smollett's motion was as follows:

"That, in the opinion of this House, the advice given to the Crown by Her Majesty's late Ministers to dismiss the last Parliament upon the 26th January last, in an abrupt manner and without any previous warning, at a time when both Houses had been summoned to meet for the despatch of public business, and when no emergency had arisen for such a step, is censurable; and further, that the precipitate appeal to the Constituencies consequent on such Dissolution is opposed to the spirit of the Constitution."

In explaining his motion, Mr. Smollett said:

". . . he (Mr. Smollett) would at once declare that if the House was not prepared to condemn the act as it ought to be condemned; if, in point of fact, it was not determined to take some legislative action in the matter, then they would be doing their best to establish a precedent of the worst possible character—a precedent which future unscrupulous Ministers—if we ever had such things—would not fail to avail themselves of at the earliest opportunity . . . He could not see why a Bill should not be introduced with the consent of Her Majesty's Ministers, requiring that in future when any General Election was brought about by surprise, and without previous notice, no writ should be issued for five or six days after the publication of the Proclamation in the *Gazette*." 218 *Hansard* (Commons) 3 s., 1101, 1106-1112.

[112] 218 *Hansard* (Commons) 3 s., 1129.

[113] Mr. MacDonald's motion mentioned that the House of Commons should condemn, among other things, "the decision of the Government to leave millions of British people in want in order to fight an election on an undisclosed scheme of tariffs and Imperial preference, conceived by sections of capitalists in their own interests, the effect of which must be to increase the cost of living and encourage the formation of anti-social trusts and combines." 168 *H. C. Deb.* 5 s., 461, 572-5.

any change in the relationship between the government and Parliament, since the government, having announced the dissolution, would wait for the decision of the electorate rather than for that of the House of Commons to determine whether it should resign.

Thus, the House of Commons, and chiefly the Opposition in the House of Commons,[114] in order to exert some influence in the determination of a dissolution, may launch a vote of lack of confidence; if such vote is passed, it is for the ministry to decide whether a dissolution is preferable to any other course. After a dissolution has been decided upon by the Cabinet and announced in Parliament, the House, or the Opposition, if it considers that the ministry in resorting to dissolution has acted unwisely, may register a Vote of Censure. Whether this vote, if passed, will lead to a resignation of the ministry depends upon the circumstances. The resignation of the Peel Government in 1835 is the only instance since 1832 in which resignation took place as a result of such a vote, which was, however, combined with an adverse vote on other matters.

Reference has already been made to Queen Victoria's suggestion of dissolution of Parliament at the Liberal Government's defeat in the House of Lords on the second reading of the Franchise Bill on July 8, 1884. Mr. Gladstone, the Prime Minister, replied that at no period of English history had the House of Commons been dissolved at the call of the House of Lords, given through an adverse vote.[115] With regard to that Franchise Bill, Lord Salisbury,[116] the leader of

---

[114] Outside of Parliament the Opposition may, under unusual circumstances, precipitate a dissolution. Regarding party activities in the later part of 1910, 1922 and 1931 which helped to precipitate dissolutions in those years, see *infra*, pp. 86-92.

[115] See *supra*, pp. 47-48.

[116] Lord Salisbury, in his letter to Lord Carnarvon of February 20, 1872, expressed his opinion for the rejection of the Ballot Bill on its

the Opposition, speaking at Chelsea on March 12, 1884, a week after the Liberal Government's plan had been announced in the House of Commons, stated that he and his friends regarded the issue raised as of such grave constitutional importance as to demand an appeal to the country before it was decided in both Houses of Parliament. When Lord Cairnes moved in the House of Lords an amendment to the second reading of the Franchise Bill insisting upon redistribution of Parliamentary seats as a necessary adjunct to an extension of the franchise in Counties, Lord Salisbury further said (on July 8) that:[117]

We have no fear of the humiliation with which we are threatened. We do not shrink from bowing to the opinion of the people, whatever that opinion may be. If it is their judgment that there should be enfranchisement without redistribution, I

second reading in the House of Lords and his views on the Lords' right to force a dissolution by saying that:

"The plan which I prefer is frankly to acknowledge that the nation is master, though the House of Commons is not, and to yield our own opinion only when the judgment of the nation has been challenged at the polls and decidedly expressed. This Doctrine, it seems to me, has the advantage of being: (1) theoretically sound, (2) popular, (3) safe against agitation and (4) so rarely applicable as practically to place little fetter upon our independence."

The Ballot Bill had been rejected by the Lords in 1870 and in 1871, and if Lord Salisbury had had his way, would have been thrown out again in 1872 [Allyn, *Lords Versus Commons* (Philadelphia, 1931), p. 100].

Lord Salisbury's assertion of the power of the Lords to compel an appeal to the country as a necessary counterweight in legislation was again expressed briefly in a correspondence with Queen Victoria towards the close of the elections in 1892. He said:

"The object of their existence (the Peers' privilege of appeal to the constituencies and their duty to exercise it) is to be a check upon hasty legislation, and the action of a check is necessarily displeasing to the persons checked. Of course, this would not justify them in setting themselves against the clear and deliberate judgment of the country, but this mistake they have never committed." Lady Gwendolen Cecil, *Life of Robert Marquis of Salisbury*, vol. iv (London, 1932), p. 169.

[117] *Cf. ibid.*, vol. iii (London, 1931), pp. 107-10, 116-124.

should be very much surprised; but I should not attempt to dispute their decision . . . I feel that we are bound, as guardians of their interests, to call upon the Government to appeal to the people and by the result of that appeal we will abide.

This claim was vehemently disputed by Mr. Gladstone as a novel attempt to usurp authority in resistance to which he was prepared to make any sacrifice. The dispute was avoided through the agreement between the Government and Opposition leaders in both Houses upon the replacement of the threat of a dictated Redistribution Bill of uncertain enactment by an agreed Bill whose provisions the Government were to be pledged beforehand to pass into law as a condition for the Peers to release the Franchise Bill. The issue between the claim of the Lords to appeal to the country and the denial, however, as Leonard Courtney remarked, remained unsettled.[118]   There was not, in fact, until 1909 any dissolution of Parliament occasioned by a vote of the House of Lords.   No government, by whatever party formed, has ever recognized in the House of Lords the right or the power to dictate a dissolution[119] because, while the prerogative of dissolution may be exercised for the purpose of getting rid of a deadlock between the two houses, another prerogative,

[118] Courtney, *The Working Constitution of the United Kingdom* (New York, 1910), pp. 41-42.

According to Francis Holland, " if the House of Lords had made good their right to reject a Budget by a victory at the General Election of January, 1910, one of two results must have followed. Liberal Governments in the future must either, when their budgets were rejected by the Lords, have introduced others with the clauses to which objection had been taken omitted, and this in effect would be to allow the Lords to amend a Budget and to force their own system of taxation on the people . . . or else the power of the House of Lords, themselves indissoluble, to dissolve the House of Commons would have been successfully asserted." May and Holland, *The Constitutional History of England* (London, 1912), vol. iii (by Holland), pp. 352-353.

[119] Mr. Asquith's Speech in the House of Commons on February 22, 1909. 1 *H. C. Deb.* 5 s., 458-459.

that of the creation of Peers, may also be resorted to in order to coerce the House of Lords into giving way to the House of Commons. Because of the existence of the latter prerogative, the House of Lords does not often refuse to give effect to the will of the House of Commons.[120] The only occasion since 1832 on which the upper House has attempted to call, and succeeded in calling, a dissolution of the House of Commons was when the former defeated on November 30, 1909 the Finance Bill by a vote of 350 to 75 and agreed to the following Resolution:[121]

This House is not justified in giving its consent to this Bill until it has been submitted to the judgment of the country.

In response to this resolution, Mr. Asquith, the Prime Minister, proposed on December 2, 1909, in the House of Commons the Motion that[122]

the action of the House of Lords in refusing to pass into law the financial provision made by this House for the Service of the Year is a breach of the Constitution and a usurpation of the rights of the Commons.

This motion was carried by a vote of 349 to 134. The first tactical victory thus having been won by Mr. Asquith,[123] he advised dissolution. Since the General Election which followed left the Liberal Government in office,[124] the action

---

[120] *Cf.* the debate between Mr. Asquith, the Prime Minister, on the one hand and Mr. Balfour and Sir Robert Finlay on the other in the House of Commons on March 24 and March 31, 1910. 15 *H. C. Deb.* 5 s., 1170-1173, 1187-1188, 1474-1475.

[121] 4 *H. L. Deb.* 5 s., 1342-1346.

[122] 13 *H. C. Deb.* 5 s., 546-582.

[123] Lee, *King Edward VII*, vol. ii, pp. 668-669.

[124] The Earl of Oxford and Asquith, *Fifty Years of British Parliament*, vol. ii, p. 92:

" If the Independent Nationalists, who were an uncertain factor, were

of the House of Lords might be considered to have been condemned by the country. The Parliament Act of 1911, passed after another appeal to the country, finally gave statutory effect to the inferior position of the House of Lords in regard to Finance and other bills. Since the solution of a deadlock between the two Houses is well provided for,[125] there seems to be very little possibility that the House of Lords can or will compel a dissolution, and hence the power of the ministry to create Peers may also be considered to be superfluous.

In recapitulation, it may suffice to say that the power of dissolution is a royal prerogative, recognized and regulated by statutes and by constitutional custom. It is exercised by the sovereign only on the advice and at the request of his ministers, or to be more specific, generally of his Prime Minister with the previous consent of the Cabinet as a whole. As a collective responsibility is implied in the fact that dissolution is usually submitted to the Cabinet for ultimate decision, the House of Commons, by way of sanctioning that responsibility, may, although it very seldom does, censure the government for advice for dissolution or for the omission of such an act and thus cause its own dissolution or the government's resignation. On the other hand, the ministry may, if it is deemed necessary, threaten a dissolution in order to secure parliamentary support and efficiency in carrying on the business of government. In a word, Parliament is dissolved by the Prime Minister with the approval of the Cabinet and the sanction of the sovereign at the risk of a Vote of Censure by the House of Commons. The possi-

---

left out of the account, this would give a majority against the mainten-ance of the Lords' veto of about 112 (385 against 273). If Ireland as a whole were left entirely out of the account, the majority against the Lords' veto in Great Britain would work out at sixty-two (315 against 253)."

[125] The Parliament Act, 1911, 1 & 2 Geo. 5, c. 13.

bility of such a vote is, however, minimized by the fear of a dissolution by the Prime Minister.[126]

[126] It should be recalled that the resignation of the Peel government in 1835 was the only occasion since 1832 on which the downfall of a government was caused by a Vote of Censure on dissolution (together with defeats on other matters). In the newly elected House of Commons the Peel government was in a minority. Yet, when it had defeated the government on the election of a speaker and on the Amendment to the Address (censuring the government on dissolution) there spread a fear that, "instead of resignation, Sir Robert Peel would try another dissolution." And "he kept the idea before the House, though in a covert manner" until he actually resigned. *The Croker Papers* (London, 1884), vol. ii, p. 266.

CHAPTER III

WHY PARLIAMENTS WERE DISSOLVED

BEFORE the year 1867 it was possible to effect the dissolution of Parliament in three ways: through the demise of the Crown, the efflux of the legal term, or the exercise of the prerogative. We have already seen that the practice of dissolution because of the demise of the Crown was abolished by the Representation of the People Act of 1867,[1] so that since that time Parliament has been dissolved on only two grounds. Since 1832 the only occasion when Parliament was dissolved by the death of the sovereign was in 1837. Two days after the death of William IV (on June 20, 1837) the two Houses of Parliament were notified through a message from Queen Victoria, the successor to William IV, that:[2]

the present state of public business, and the period of the Session, when considered in connexion with the law that imposes upon her Majesty the duty of summoning a new Parliament, within a limited time, renders it inexpedient, in the judgment of her Majesty, that any new measure should be recommended for your adoption, with the exception of such as may be requisite for carrying on the public service from the close of the present Session to the meeting of the new Parliament.

And on July 17, the Parliament was formally dissolved.[3]

Among the dissolutions, since the passing of the Reform

[1] See *supra*, p. 57, fn. 99.

[2] 38 *Hansard* (Lords) 3 s., 1546-1554; 38 *Hansard* (Commons) 3 s., 1554-1564.

[3] 38 *Hansard* (Lords) 3 s., 1919-1922.

Bill in 1832, those in 1847,[4] 1865,[5] 1880,[6] 1892[7], 1918,[8] and 1929[9] took place mainly on account of the near efflux of the legal duration of Parliament.[10]   It should be observed, however, that none of the Parliaments dissolved in those years continued up to the last day allowed by the law.[11]   The term of the Parliament dissolved on July 6, 1865 was 329 days and that dissolved on March 24, 1880 was 346 days short of the maximum duration prescribed by the Septennial Act of 1716, although both Parliaments were distinguished as being the only Parliaments since 1832 which ever attained their seventh sessions under that act.   The Parliament dissolved on November 25, 1918, two weeks after the Armistice which removed the possibility for any further extension of the term of Parliament, was sixty-six days short of the eight-year period which that Parliament was legally entitled

[4] *Letters of Queen Victoria, 1837–1861,* vol. ii, p. 142; *Annual Register,* 1847, Chronicle, p. 95.

[5] 180 *Hansard* (Lords) 3 s., 1178-1183.

[6] 251 *Hansard* (Lords) 3 s., 1268-1270.

[7] Lady Gwendolen Cecil, *Life of Robert Marquis of Salisbury,* vol. iv, pp. 397-403.

[8] Churchill, *The World Crisis, the Aftermath* (London, 1929), pp. 39-41.

[9] *Annual Register,* 1929, English History, pp. 1, 40-41.

[10] In advising a dissolution on September 5, 1900, Lord Salisbury mentioned to Queen Victoria the near-efflux of time as one of the reasons for rendering such advice (*Letters of Queen Victoria, 1886–1901,* vol. iii, p. 586), although the Parliament might have existed nearly two more years.

[11] According to the *Constitutional Year Book,* 1933, p. 138, the duration of those parliaments was as follows:

Parliaments Dissolved on		Years	Days
23 July,	1847	5	337
6 July,	1865	6	36
24 March,	1880	6	19
28 June,	1892	5	328
25 Nov.,	1918	7	299
10 May,	1929	4	159

to exist. And finally the Parliament dissolved on May 10, 1929, which is so far the only Parliament dissolved because of the efflux of time under the Parliament Act of 1911 was 206 days short of the five-year period prescribed by that Act.

Turning now to dissolution of Parliament through the exercise of the prerogative, the most common ground for resorting to a dissolution, especially during the nineteenth century, was the assumption that the House of Commons did not correctly represent the opiniòns and wishes of the nation. " Ever since 1784, it has been completely established, as the rule of the Constitution, that when the House of Commons refuses its confidence to the ministers of the Crown, the question whether in doing so, it has correctly expressed the opinion of the country, may properly be tested by a dissolution." [12]   It may therefore, be appropriate for us to sketch briefly, first of all, the cases of dissolution due to a defeat in the House of Commons since the Reform of 1832.

On May 18, 1841, the Melbourne Government was defeated by a majority of 36 (with 281 for and 317 against the government) on Lord Sandon's Amendment of the government's proposal for reducing the duties on sugar.[13]   The Cabinet, after several discussions, decided on dissolution in preference to immediate resignation in order to secure a verdict of the country on the question of the Corn Laws. " It was thought best, however, for the sake of the convenient despatch of business, and of a Constitutional regard on the part of the Crown towards the House of Commons, to defer the announcement of this resolution." [14]   Accordingly on May 20, Lord John Russell, the Chancellor of the Exchequer, announced that on May 24, he would move that the House resolve itself into a Committee of Ways and Means, with a

[12] Todd, *On Parliamentary Government in England*, vol. ii, p. 506.

[13] 58 *Hansard* (Commons) 3 s., 561-673.

[14] Russell, *Recollections and Suggestions, 1813-1873*, pp. 206-8.

view to moving the usual Sugar Duties therein. On being questioned he further announced that he intended to bring forward the question of the corn laws. This announcement occasioned much astonishment in the crowded House since the Members had expected " to hear some intimation of resignation or an explanation of the cause of not resigning." [15] On May 27, Sir Robert Peel, the Leader of the Opposition, " who was not aware of the intention of the Cabinet ",[16] moved a vote of want of confidence which, after a long debate, was carried on June 4 by a majority of one (with 311 for and 312 against the government.) [17] Three days later, dissolution was announced in the House of Commons,[18] and Parliament was dissolved on June 23.

Between 1841 and 1857 there was no dissolution of Parliament directly due to a withdrawal of confidence by the House of Commons. On March 3 of the latter year, the Palmerston Government was defeated by a majority of 16 (with 247 for and 263 against the government) on the Resolution moved by Mr. Cobden condemning the government for its policy in carrying on the war in China.[19] By accepting the challenge of Mr. Disraeli that he appeal to the country, the Prime Minister announced to the House, the next day but one, that as soon as the necessary business could be completed, Parliament would be dissolved.[20]

On March 31, two years later, the Derby Government was defeated by a majority of 39 (with 291 for and 330 against the government) on the second reading of the Representation

[15] 58 *Hansard* (Commons) 3 s., 676.

[16] Russell, *op. cit.*, p. 234.

[17] 58 *Hansard* (Commons) 3 s., 803-889, 1121-1247.

[18] *Ibid.*, 1265.

[19] 144 *Hansard* (Commons) 3 s., 1722-1850.

[20] *Ibid.*, 1894-1897; 144 *Hansard* (Lords) 3 s., 1885-1886; Ashley, *Life of Viscount Palmerston* (London, 1876), vol. ii, pp. 134-135.

of the People Bill.[21] " Though the Parliament was little
more than a couple of years old, yet in face of the desperate
confusion among leaders, parties, and groups, and upon the
plea that reform had not been formally submitted as an issue
to the country, Lord Derby felt justified in dissolving " Parliament.[22] The dissolution was announced in Parliament on
April 4, after Queen Victoria had given her sanction to the
advice of dissolution in preference to acceptance of resignation, which was submitted as an alternative course which the
Queen might choose.[23]

Hardly had a decade elapsed when Parliament was again
dissolved because of an adverse vote in the House of Commons.   On April 30, 1868 the Disraeli Government was defeated by a majority of 65 (with 265 for and 330 against the
government) in the Committee on the Resolution moved by
Mr. Gladstone for the disestablishment of the Irish Church.[24]
The Prime Minister immediately moved adjournment on the
ground that the vote had altered the relation between the
government and the House; and proceeded on the next morning to tender to the Queen advice for dissolution, with resignation as an alternative.   The dissolution was sanctioned by
the Queen on May 2, in preference to an acceptance of resignation,[25] and announced by the Earl of Malmesbury and Mr.
Disraeli in the House of Lords and the House of Commons
respectively on May 4.[26]

The next case of dissolution on account of a withdrawal of
confidence by the House of Commons occurred eighteen years

[21] 153 *Hansard* (Commons) 3 s., 1157-1264.

[22] Morley, *Life of Gladstone,* vol. i, pp. 621-2.

[23] 153 *Hansard* (Lords) 3 s., 1264-1291 ; 153 *Hansard* (Commons) 3 s.,
1301-1307.

[24] 191 *Hansard* (Commons) 3 s., 1583-1679.

[25] Monypenny and Buckle, *Life of Disraeli,* vol. v, pp. 30-32.

[26] 191 *Hansard* (Lords) 3 s., 1686; 191 *Hansard* (Commons) 3 s.,
1694-1708.

later. At an early hour on June 8, 1886, the Gladstone Government was defeated by a majority of 30 (with 311 for and 341 against the government) on the second reading of the Government of Ireland Bill.[27] Despite the fact that a General Election had taken place only six months before, the government, upon the insistence of Mr. Gladstone, decided in favor of dissolution,[28] to which the Queen gave her sanction " on the condition that it was to be done at once." [29]

The only occasion since 1886 of a dissolution of Parliament on the withdrawal of confidence by the House of Commons was in 1924. In October of the latter year, the Conservative Opposition through Sir Robert Horne moved a Vote of Censure on the Labour Government's " conduct in relation to the institution and subsequent withdrawal of criminal proceedings against the editor of the ' Worker's Weekly.' " To this vote the Liberals (who held the balance of power) proposed, through Sir John Simon, an amendment providing that " a Select Committee be appointed to investigate and report upon the circumstances leading up " to that withdrawal. Because Mr. Baldwin, the Conservative Leader, in the midst of the debate unexpectedly instructed the Conservative rank and file to support the Liberal Amendment, the Amendment was passed on October 8 by a majority of 166 (with 198 for and 364 against the Government) while the Vote of Censure was defeated by a majority of 161 (with 359 for and 198 against the government.) [30] Because of this defeat in the House of Commons, the Mac-Donald Government resorted to dissolution which was sanc-

[27] 306 *Hansard* (Commons) 3 s., 1145-1245.

[28] Morley, *op. cit.*, vol. iii, pp. 341-342.

[29] *Letters of Queen Victoria, 1886-1901*, vol. i, p. 143. *Cf.* further *ibid.*, vol. i, pp. 143-5; 306 *Hansard* (Lords) 3 s., 1254; 306 *Hansard* (Commons) 3 s., 1304-1306.

[30] 177 *H. C. Deb.* 5 s., 581-704.

tioned by King George V and announced in Parliament on October 9.[31]

In brief, during the hundred years under discussion (1832-1931) there have been only six dissolutions directly due to the withdrawal of confidence by the House of Commons. The first five took place within the fifty-year period after Queen Victoria ascended the English throne (1837-1886). Since the great Liberal defeat at the polls in 1886, the House of Commons has " voted " out, so to speak, its existence only once. And among the six cases, that of 1841 was occasioned first by a defeat on the Budget and then by a vote of want of confidence. A vote of censure for commission or omission of an act might also cause a dissolution of Parliament.[32] Thus, Parliament was dissolved in 1857 because of a Vote of Censure on the government's policy regarding the China War and again in 1924 because of the Vote of Censure on the government's conduct regarding the institution and subsequent withdrawal of the Campbell Case. On the other hand, the dissolution of 1868 might be regarded as the result of the Vote of Censure on the government's failure to adopt the policy of disestablishing the Irish Church. Finally, defeat of government measures might also serve as a ground for dissolution. Thus, the defeat on the Representation of The People Bill caused a dissolution in

[31] *Ibid.*, 731; 59 *H. C. Deb.* 5 s., 667.

The real issue on which the Labour Government was defeated was the Russian treaties, although the question on which a Vote of Censure was passed concerned its conduct in relation to the instituting and subsequent withdrawal of criminal proceedings against a Communist named Campbell, the editor of *The Worker's Weekly*. Tiltman, *James Ramsay Mac-Donald, Labour's Man of Destiny* (4th edition, London), p. 184. *Cf.* further *Annual Register,* 1924, English History, pp. 103 *et seq.*

[32] A vote of want of confidence differs from a Vote of Censure in the fact that it declares that the House of Commons has "no confidence in an administration, without assigning their reasons for such declaration." Todd, *On Parliamentary Government in England*, vol. ii, p. 493.

1859, and that on the Government of Ireland Bill brought about another in 1886.

We pass now from governments placed in a minority by a vote of the House of Commons to consider the action taken by those governments which have been in a minority on assuming office. There have been ten such since 1832. Of these five chose to dissolve rather than to attempt to carry on the business of administration.[33] The tendency to appeal to the people almost immediately was especially marked where the Parliament had existed for a considerable length of time before the minority government was formed.[34]

[33] The Russell Government formed in July, 1846 preferred to carry on the government rather than to dissolve Parliament despite minority support in the House of Commons. The same course was pursued by Lord Derby in 1859 and by Lord Derby and Disraeli in 1866-1868. The actions of Lord Derby and Disraeli might be justified by the fact that in both cases the Parliament, in which the government formed by the opposition party had been defeated, had existed for only a few months when they assumed office. Hence, a dissolution in each case would have been incompatible with the spirit of the Constitution according to which frequent dissolutions ought to be avoided. In the case of the Russell Government, however, although dissolution might be resorted to immediately following the assumption of office, on the ground of near-efflux of the legal term, since the Parliament had been in existence almost five years, yet such a step was not taken until a year later.

Under the three-party system the Labour Governments of 1924 and 1929-1931, although in a minority, counted on Liberal support for the majority in the House of Commons. Dissolution was out of the question when Mr. MacDonald formed the Labour Government after Mr. Baldwin's resignation in 1924 as a result of the defeat in the new House of Commons and in 1929 as a result of an appeal to the electorate.

[34] Note in the third column of the following table the approximate time in terms of years and months that the Parliament had existed when the minority government assumed office:

Opening of the First Session of Parliament	Assumption of Office by Minority Gov't.	Interval between Years	Months
Jan. 29, 1833	Dec. 26, 1834	1	11
Nov. 18, 1847	Feb. 27, 1852	4	3
Apr. 29, 1880	June 24, 1885	5	2
Aug. 4, 1892	July 2, 1895	2	11
Dec. 3, 1900	Dec. 5, 1905	5	

In 1834, when William IV dismissed Lord Melbourne and summoned the minority leader, Sir Robert Peel, to form a government, Parliament was not in session. Dissolution having been decided upon before his arrival in England from Rome, the new Prime Minister, immediately upon his assumption of office, appealed to the country without even meeting the Parliament.

On February 20, 1852, the Russell Government was defeated by a majority of 11 (with 125 for and 136 against the government) on Lord Palmerston's amendment (to the motion proposed by the government) in favor of re-organizing the "regular" instead of raising a "local" Militia.[35] As a result, the Russell Government resigned.[36] Lord Derby, the minority leader, succeeded in forming a government by promising to confine himself during the session to business already launched and advanced, or of an urgent character, and to advise, as soon as he could, for dissolution. This advice was finally given in July 1852.[37]

The Gladstone Government resigned in 1885, as a result[38] of its defeat on June 8 by a majority of 12 (with 252 for and 264 against the government) on the second reading of the Customs and Inland Revenue Bill.[39] If Lord Salisbury, the leader of the Opposition, took office he could only do so by grace of Mr. Gladstone, the leader of the majority whom he had just defeated. After some delay, Lord Salisbury, having through the Queen received assurance that he would not be embarrassed in office, formed the so-called "government of care-takers" to wind up the Parliament and go to

---

[35] 119 *Hansard* (Commons) 3 s., 838-876.

[36] *Letters of Queen Victoria, 1837–1861*, vol. ii, pp. 444-446; 119 *Hansard* (Lords) 3 s., 882-885; 119 *Hansard* (Commons) 3 s., 887-888.

[37] Morley, *Life of Gladstone*, vol. i, pp. 424-425.

[38] *Letters of Queen Victoria, 1862–1885*, vol. iii, p. 658; 298 *Hansard* (Lords) 3 s., 1521-1522; 298 *Hansard* (Commons) 3 s., 1528-1531.

[39] *Ibid.*, 1417-1515.

the country.[40]   The Parliament was accordingly dissolved in November, 1885.

Upon the resignation of the Rosebery Government [41] because of its defeat on June 21, 1895 by a majority of 7 (with 125 for and 132 against the government) on the Army Estimates,[42] Lord Salisbury, the leader of the minority, although quite ready to form a government, advised the Queen that Lord Rosebery, and not he, ought to dissolve.[43]   On being informed of Lord Salisbury's opinion, Lord Rosebery considered, as Sir Arthur Bigge wrote to Lord Salisbury on June 25, 1895, that: [44]

as he (Lord Rosebery) has resigned, and his resignation has been accepted, it would be necessary to consult his colleagues, should you (Lord Salisbury) address any formal objection to the course he has adopted, or declare your unwillingness to form a Government.

Since the Queen did not wish " to prolong matters by such negotiations," Lord Salisbury, whose government had been defeated in the same Parliament three years before,[45] accepted office after having obtained an assurance from Lord Rosebery that the Liberal majority in the House of Commons would co-operate in completing the urgent business of the session,

[40] *Letters of Queen Victoria, 1862–1885,* vol. iii, pp. 657 *et seq.;* 298 *Hansard* (Lords) 3 s., 1631-1636.

[41] *Letters of Queen Victoria, 1886–1901,* vol. ii, pp. 521-522; 34 *Hansard* (Lords) 4 s., 1742; 34 *Hansard* (Commons) 4 s., 1746-1748.

[42] *Ibid.,* 1673-1712.

[43] *Letters of Queen Victoria, op. cit.,* vol. ii, pp. 524-525.

[44] *Ibid.,* vol. ii, pp. 525-526.

[45] On August 11, 1892, the Salisbury Government was defeated by a majority of 40 (with 310 for the 350 against the government) on a vote of want of confidence, on the adoption of an Amendment, proposed by Mr. Asquith, to the Address in reply to the Speech from the throne. [7 *Hansard* (Commons) 4 s., 433-446.] As a result, it resigned. *Letters of Queen Victoria, op. cit.,* vol. ii, p. 140; 7 *Hansard* (Lords) 4 s., 447.

and would make ready the way for an early dissolution.[46] This took place in July, 1895.

Toward the end of 1905 the Balfour Government which, since 1903, had been greatly weakened by the resignation of five ministers, including Joseph Chamberlain and the Duke of Devonshire, owing to difference of opinion on the fiscal issue,[47] was confronted with increasing difficulties. It was subjected to constant attacks in the House of Commons,[48] and sustained the loss of several by-elections in the country.[49] In spite of the Prime Minister's emphasis on the necessity of unity on a moderate policy of fiscal reform, his appeal proved ineffective.[50] The "members of the Cabinet were . . . openly debating with each other as to the part which Tariff Reform should play in Unionist policy." As a consequence, Balfour resigned instead of dissolving Parliament, presumably to put the opposition at a disadvantage by casting upon it the responsibility of government.[51] Campbell-Bannerman, the leader of the minority, formed a government " on condition that there was an immediate dissolution of Parlia-

[46] Whates, *The Third Salisbury Administration, 1895–1900* (Westminister, undated), pp. 4-5.

[47] Raymond, *Mr. Balfour, A Biography* (London, 1920), pp. 94-114. Cf. *Fiscal Reform, Speeches delivered by A. J. Balfour from June 1800 to December 1905* (London, 1906), especially pp. 59 *et seq.*

[48] Lowther, *A Speaker's Commentaries* (London, 1925), vol. ii, pp. 4-6; 11-12.

[49] Spender, *Life of Sir Henry Campbell-Bannerman* (London, 1923), vol. ii, p. 190.

[50] Griffith-Boscawen, *Fourteen Years in Parliament* (London, 1907), pp. 347-349; Lee, *King Edward VII*, vol. ii, pp. 188 *et seq.*

[51] Spender, *op. cit.*, vol. ii, pp. 188-191.
Bernard Holland, the author of *Life of the Duke of Devonshire*, commented upon the Balfour resignation by saying:
"Resignation of a Government who still had a large majority in the House of Commons, and had suffered no decisive defeat in a division was without precedent. But the majority on the leading question of the day was not real or sound, and more than once the Prime Minister had only escaped defeat by avoiding battle." *Life of Spencer Compton* (London, 1911), vol. ii, p. 390.

ment." [52] This condition was complied with in January, 1906.

Among the five cases just described the Peel Government, formed at the end of 1834, appealed to the electorate without meeting Parliament at all, while the other four governments convened Parliament only for the purpose of winding up the business before dissolution was effected. Incidentally, in three of the five cases, the downfall of the government, which ultimately led to the formation of a new government and dissolution of Parliament by the minority, was caused by a vote in the House of Commons. Thus, there were nine cases—the three cases just mentioned (1852, 1885, and 1895) together with the six cases described above (1841, 1857, 1859, 1868, 1886 and 1924)—in which dissolution was caused either directly or indirectly by a vote in the House of Commons. All of them except that of 1924 occurred in the nineteenth century. Since the Conservative victory at the polls in 1895 there has been only one occasion when the cause of the dissolution might be traced to a defeat in the House of Commons. An analysis of the nature of the votes in the nine cases reveals that on three occasions the votes registered defeats of the government either on Appropriations or on Supply. In the former category fall the votes of 1841 and 1885 and in the latter that of 1859. The Dissolution of 1841, which had been decided upon after the government's defeat on the proposal for the reduction of sugar duties, was actually not resorted to, however, until a vote of want of confidence was passed by the House of Commons. In 1857 and 1924 the votes which caused the dissolutions of Parliament were distinctly Votes of Censure. Although the vote on the Resolution for the Disestablishment of the Irish Church, proposed in 1868 by Mr. Gladstone, the leader of the Opposition, might in a way, as already remarked,

[52] Grey, *Twenty-Five years, 1892–1916* (New York, 1925), vol. i, pp. 59 *et seq.*

be regarded as a Vote of Censure, it should properly be considered as belonging in another category. For, the passage of such a Resolution amounted to a grant of leave to private members to introduce bills of a constitutional character, notwithstanding the opposition of ministers.[53] Finally on the other three occasions, the defeats were either on government bills or on government resolutions asking leave to bring in a bill. Thus, as we have noted, the dissolutions of 1859 and 1886 were due to the defeats on the Representation of the People Bill and the Government of Ireland Bill respectively, while the vote against the Russell Government in 1852 on the proposal that " leave be given to bring in a Bill to amend the Laws respecting the Local Militia " was accountable for the dissolution by the Opposition which later formed a Government.

From dissolutions due to defeats in the House of Commons we may now turn our attention to those produced by other causes. It will be obvious from what has been said in previous sections of this monograph that the actions of the sovereign and the House of Lords are of no great importance in this connection. Since the establishment of the idea of ministerial responsibility these partners of the Commons in the process of law-making have seldom demanded and still less often caused a dissolution. Indeed, it may be permissible to recall, only in 1834, when William IV dismissed the Melbourne Government, has the sovereign precipitated a dissolution; and the only occasion on which the

[53] Todd in his *On Parliamentary Government in England* (vol. ii, pp. 492-493, 502-503), mentioned five possible ways by which the withdrawal of confidence could be effected. The summary here is based largely upon a classification such as he made. Those five ways are: (1) a direct vote of want of confidence, (2) censure of certain specified acts or omissions, (3) rejection of some legislative measure proposed by ministers, the acceptance of which by Parliament they have declared to be of vital importance, (4) the determination of Parliament to enact a particular law contrary to the advice and consent of the administration and (5) defeat of financial estimates proposed by the ministry.

House of Lords has asked for a dissolution was in 1909 at the time of its refusal to pass the Lloyd George budget.

Far more significant is the tightening of party control upon the members of Parliament—a development which may almost be said to threaten the underlying principle of the English Parliamentary system, the responsibility of the Cabinet to the House of Commons. Since the development of party organizations in the seventies of the last century, most of the members of Parliament have been furnished by the two, and later three, political parties. In the House of Commons, ordinary members have to a large extent lost their independence of action; they have voted and walked into the division lobbies usually under the direction of the parliamentary Whips. The House of Commons itself has thus declined to the status of a political machine to register party decisions arrived at outside Westminster Hall. Furthermore, the general tendency since 1900 seems to be such that party decisions and Cabinet resolutions decided upon because of reasons of party strategy have tended to supersede House of Commons votes in determining the government of the day either to resign or to request dissolution. This conclusion we shall seek to illustrate at the outset by re-examining briefly the nine cases where, as we have already seen, dissolutions of Parliament were caused either directly or indirectly by votes in the House of Commons. We find that party oscillations of one kind or another played a considerable part in those votes. Thus, the defeats of governments in 1841,[54] 1852 (Russell),[55] 1857 [56] and 1886 [57] might

[54] *Cf.* Clark, *Peel and the Conservative Party* (London, 1929), pp. 473, 481-482; 57 *Hansard* (Commons) 3 s., 1252-1279; 58 *Hansard* (Commons) 3 s., 673.

[55] Ashley, *Life of Viscount Palmerston*, vol. i, pp. 333-335. *Cf. Memoirs of Baron Stockmar*, vol. ii, pp. 445-450; Monypenny and Buckle, *Life of Disraeli*, vol. iii, pp. 282-6; *Letters of Queen Victoria, 1837-1861*, vol. ii, pp. 346-352.

[56] *Cf.* Wolf, *Life of Lord Ripon* (London, 1921), vol. i, pp. 98-99; Ashley, *op. cit.*, vol. ii, pp. 134-135.

[57] *Cf.* Morley, *Life of Gladstone*, vol. iii, pp. 301-341.

be attributed to the defections of the government majority or a split of the party in power, while the breach between Whigs and Radicals was partially responsible for the downfall of the Gladstone Government in 1885.[58] In 1859[59] and 1868,[60] the defeats of the Conservative Governments were occasioned by the reunion of dissentient sections of the Liberal majority in Opposition. Finally, defeats of government were sometimes caused by the withdrawal of support by third parties. This was true of the government defeats in 1895[61] and in 1924[62] through the withdrawal of support by the Nationalists and Liberals respectively, while an alliance between the Nationalists and Tories, together with the breach between the Whigs and Radicals, resulted in an adverse vote for the Gladstone Government in 1885.[63] But what should be stressed is the fact that between 1832 and 1900 there was no instance in which Parliament was dissolved as the direct result of exertion of party influence alone.[64] Whatever underlying influence the shifting of party alignment might have on the duration of Parliament, there was

[58] *Cf.* Winston S. Churchill, *Lord Randolph Churchill* (New York, 1906), vol. i, pp. 398-399; Lee, *King Edward VII*, vol. i, p. 522; Morley, *op. cit.*, vol. iii, pp. 200-203.

[59] *Cf.* Elliot, *Life of Lord Goschen* (London, 1911), vol. i, pp. 55-56; Maxwell, *Life and Letters of the Fourth Earl of Clarendon* (London, 1913), vol. ii, pp. 178-179.

[60] *Cf.* 191 *Hansard* (Commons) 3 s., 837-945; Monypenny and Buckle, *Life of Disraeli*, vol. v, pp. 2 *et seq.;* Morley, *op. cit.*, vol. ii, pp. 245-247.

[61] Spender, *Life of Sir Henry Campbell-Bannerman*, vol. i, pp. 161-162. *Cf.* The Earl of Oxford and Asquith, *Fifty Years of British Parliament*, vol. i, p. 261; Whates, *The Third Salisbury Administration, 1895-1900*, pp. 2-3; Raymond, *Life of Lord Rosebery* (New York, 1923), pp. 130 *et seq.*

[62] *Cf.* The Liberal Magazine, vol. 32, no. 374, pp. 640, 644-645, November, 1924; *Annual Register*, 1924, English History, pp. 103-105.

[63] *Supra*, fn. 58.

[64] The dissolution of 1874 is but an apparent exception to this general statement. (See *infra*, pp. 95-97.)

also a vote in the House of Commons before the government was induced to dissolve. However, since the passing away of that great Commoner, Mr. Gladstone, in 1898, the practice has seemed to veer in the opposite direction. As a matter of fact, with the exception of the dissolution of 1924, no Parliament since the end of the last century has been dissolved because of a vote in the House of Commons.

The change in political attitudes suggested by the facts just mentioned may best be illustrated by a remark made by Disraeli, on the eve of the election of 1880, in reply to those who felt he should have seized the fortunate occasion of the signing of the Berlin Treaty in 1878 for an immediate appeal to the country: [65]

People insist that I should have dissolved Parliament when I came home from Berlin. To have done so would have been one of the most unconstitutional acts of the century. A minister with a large majority in the House of Commons has no business to dissolve merely with the object of gaining an advantage at the polls due to transitory circumstances. It is said I have lost a golden opportunity. I am not so sure of it. The English people do not like breaches of constitutional practice. Had I yielded to the temptation that undoubtedly presented itself in July, 1878, they might, and probably would, have visited my sins upon my head.

What had been deemed to be " one of the most unconstitutional acts " by Lord Beaconsfield in 1878 was however carried out twenty-two years later by his successor and chief lieutenant, Lord Salisbury, under similar circumstances. In spite of the support of a majority in the House of Commons —a majority even greater than that Lord Beaconsfield secured in his second administration (1874-1880) [66]—Lord

---

[65] Lucy, *A Diary of the Unionist Parliament, 1895–1900* (Bristol, 1901), pp. 349-350.

[66] According to the *Constitutional Year Book*, 1933, pp. 255-6, the

Salisbury appealed to the country in September, 1900, "before the enthusiasm of victory (in South Africa) died down." Although a General Election could have been postponed for another year or so, yet "the opportunity was too good to be thrown way." Except as being justified by the necessity of having a mandate on "the policy of annexing the Boer Republics and of suppressing all opposition by force of arms without parley," [67] an appeal without having been preceded by a defeat in the House of Commons could not be viewed otherwise than as what Lord Beaconsfield called a dissolution "merely with the object of gaining an advantage at the polls due to transitory circumstances."

Since the dissolution of 1900 Parliament has been brought to an end directly because of party influence of some sort about once every ten years. On April 14, 1910, the resolutions dealing with the relations between the two Houses of Parliament proposed by the Asquith Government were passed in the House of Commons. A Bill embodying those resolutions was introduced by the government with a firm determination that it should receive statutory enactment. In view of the sudden death of Edward VII, the leaders of the two major parties then voluntarily agreed to stop their fight and tried to settle the constitutional issue through a Joint Conference.[68] After twenty-one meetings, the Prime Minister publicly announced that the Conference had "come to an end without arriving at an agreement." [69] At that time the

returns of the General Elections of 1874 and 1895 were as follows: 1874: Conservatives, 352; Liberals, 242; and Nationals, 58. 1895: Conservatives, 341; Liberal Unionists, 70; Gladstonian Liberals, 177 and Nationalists, 82.

[67] Churchill, *A Roving Commission, My Early Life* (New York, 1930), p. 355.

[68] Earl of Oxford and Asquith, *Fifty Years of British Parliament*, vol. ii, pp. 98, 103; 20 *H. C. Deb.* 5 s., 82-87.

[69] The London *Times*, Nov. 11, 1910, p. 8.

government " might have proceeded to discuss this great
Constitutional question, ignoring the Conference altogether,
and proceeding in the ordinary way by Bill," but it felt that
" it would be a futile course, not because the Conference has
broken down, but because the two Parties in the State can
not on this subject be brought together." [70]   So it advised the
new sovereign, George V, for a dissolution with the under-
standing that " in the event of the policy of the Government
being approved by an adequate majority in the new House
of Commons, His Majesty will be ready to exercise his constitutional powers, which may involve the prerogative of
creating peers, if needed, to secure that effect shall be given
to the decision of the country."   The King, after discussing
the matter in all its bearings with Mr. Asquith and Lord
Crewe, informed them that he felt that he had no alternative
but to assent to the advice.[71]   Upon the announcement of
dissolution in the House of Commons on November 18, Mr.
Balfour, the leader of the Opposition, "as a Constitutional
critic—not as a party leader ", launched an attack on the
government, although he had, "speaking as a party, not the
slightest objection to an election."   He said: [72]

I quite agree, since the Conference has been broken down, since
party is again arrayed against party, and, as everybody knows,
a fight is probably imminent. But I do not think that that
justifies the action of the Prime Minister in giving the advice
to the Crown that he has done. He is putting Parliament in
the second place to the Conference. What happened in that
Conference rests with those who took part in it. Nothing but
the failure of the Conference is public property, or can, in my
opinion, properly be so. What is public property is the action
which takes place in this House or in the other House. . . . I

[70] 6 *H. L. Deb.* 5 s., 761.
[71] The Earl of Oxford and Asquith, *op. cit.,* vol. ii, pp. 103-104.
[72] 20 *H. C. Deb.* 5 s., 87-93.

do complain that they should have violated constitutional precedent because they are masters in this House on which depends the tenure of office of Ministers. They are, I understand, supported by a large, homogeneous, united combination. Why should they resign or dissolve? There is no reason why they should do either, and if you will look through the constitutional text books, I do not think you will find any precedent. Consider the conditions under which, in the long history of the country, it has been thought proper in the past for Ministers to advise the Sovereign to dissolve. I do not believe you will find a single case that comes within the precedent which the right Hon. Gentleman desires to set up.

Other members who followed pursued the same argument with greater stress on the breaking down of the parliamentary system of government.[78]

Long before the resignation of the Coalition Government, in October, 1922, dissatisfaction with it had been increasing in the ranks of the Conservative Party. Local associations had one by one declared their desire to be independent of the Coalition, and since the beginning of June the " Die-Hard " group of Conservatives under the leadership of Lord Salisbury, had been appealing for independence. Colonel Leslie Wilson, M.P., the Chief Unionist Whip, in his Exeter Speech on October 6, openly advocated a united Conservative Party and a greater partnership in the government. In an interview with the *Yorkshire Evening News* on October 11, he said that the return of the party system of government was essential. " Meetings of the Conservative Ministers took place on October 10th and 11th to discuss the situation, and the expediency was strongly urged upon them of terminating the Coalition before an appeal was made to the country, in order to preserve the unity of their party." Although by that time discontented Unionists were said to have outnum-

[78] *Ibid.*, 93 *et seq.*

bered the supporters of the Coalition, Mr. Chamberlain still preferred the policy of maintenance of the Coalition. When the meeting of the Conservative ministers and members of the House of Commons took place at the Carlton Club on October 19 as arranged by Mr. Chamberlain, his policy of co-operation was defeated. After Mr. Bonar Law had made a decisive speech in which he attached " more importance to keeping our party a united body than to winning the next election," the meeting, by a vote of 186 to 87, passed the resolution :

That this meeting of Conservative members of the House of Commons declares its opinion that the Conservative Party, while willing to cooperate with Coalition Liberals, fights the election as an independent party with its own leader and its own programme.

The immediate result of the defeat was that Mr. Chamberlain and other Conservative Ministers sent in their resignations to Mr. Lloyd George. The same afternoon the latter tendered his resignation to the king and advised him to send for Mr. Bonar Law who later, as Prime Minister, dissolved the Parliament.[74]

[74] The *Liberal Magazine*, vol. 30, no. 350, pp. 714-723, Nov., 1922.

Additional light has been thrown on the situation by the Earl of Ronaldshay in his *Life of Lord Curzon:*

" A meeting of the National Union of Conservative Associations had been called for November the 13th; and it was to consider whether it would be fair to the Conservative party to bring on a General Election before that date that Mr. Winston Churchill invited the Prime Minister and leading Unionist members of the Cabinet, including Lord Curzon, to dinner at his house [at which] by the end of the evening a decision had been reached . . . in favor of an appeal to the country before November the 13th." Vol. iii, p. 312.

And then the Earl of Ronaldshay continues :

" During the opening days of October the agitation in the ranks of the Conservative party had become a factor which it was impossible to ignore, and those who had agreed to an immediate dissolution were invited by Mr. Churchill to a second dinner at his house on Sunday, October

The resignation of the second Labour Government and the subsequent dissolution of Parliament in 1931, while attributable chiefly to the disagreement between the Prime Minister and Snowden on the one hand and the majority of ministers led by Henderson on the other upon the proposal of a ten per cent reduction in unemployment insurance benefits, were made possible by the active part played by the King and the resort by the Prime Minister to negotiations with leaders of opposition parties rather than to discussion in the Cabinet.   As recorded by the London *Times,* the king's decision to return to London from Balmoral August 22 " was entirely his own.   So was the determination on his arrival to see the leaders of all parties, though he properly sought and received the advice of his Prime Minister before doing so." Furthermore, during the Prime Minister's last visit to the Palace on the night of August 23, when he informed the king that the Cabinet was hopelessly divided and that no course except resignation was possible, the king " persuaded him at least to sleep over the situation and to return in the morning with the Conservative and Liberal leaders."   The con-

the 15th, to consider the position in light of it.   But by October the 15th Mr. Lloyd George had made his speech at Manchester (which had the effect of encouraging the Greeks to renew their struggle against the Turks in the Grecian-Turkish conflict of 1922; a breach was thus caused between himself and some ministers in the Coalition Cabinet), and news of his communications with the Italian Envoy (on the subject of the attitude to be adopted by the Italian delegate at the Peace conference to settle the dispute between Turkey and Greece) had reached Lord Curzon (who, though then Foreign Secretary, had no previous knowledge of them), and on the 15th, therefore, his mind was finally made up.   He could no longer agree to an immediate appeal to the country in which the Coalition including himself were to appear before the electorate as "a happy and united party."   Nor, in these circumstances, did he feel able to attend the dinner party at Mr. Churchill's house that night. . . . On Monday the 16th, he (Lord Curzon) saw Mr. Chamberlain and learned that at the dinner on the previous night it had been decided to call a meeting of Unionist members of the House of Commons to be held at the Carlton Club on Thursday the 19th."   Vol. iii, pp. 318-19.

ferences between the king and the leaders of the three parties, the Prime Minister, Mr. Baldwin and Sir Herbert Samuel, and those among the party leaders themselves on August 23 and 24 resulted in an official announcement that " the formation of a National Government is under consideration." Later, when the Prime Minister returned to Downing Street at midnight on August 24, his colleagues in the Labour Cabinet were informed of their fate.[75] So " the change of government " as Professor Laski said, " was effected without any discussion save between the party leaders ", and " the new Cabinet, in fact, was born of a Palace Revolution." [76] On August 25, when Mr. MacDonald as the Prime Minister of the new government spoke in a radio broadcast, he announced the dissolution of Parliament by saying that: [77]

It is a government . . . of individuals. It has been formed to do this work (to deal with the national emergency). If the work takes a little time, the life of the Government will be short. When that life is finished, the work of the House of Commons and the general political situation will return to where they were last week, and those who have taken risks will receive either our punishment or our reward.

The election which will follow will not be fought by the Government. There will be no coupons, and, I hope, no illegitimate prejudices.

According to this announcement and an official communique preceding it, the government, having carried through its measures for making the national accounts balance, would resign and leave party politics to resume their normal course. The later necessity, however, of abandoning the gold standard, together with the clamor of the Die-hards for tariffs, forced a dissolution by the National Government in October,

75 The London *Times*, August 24, 1931, p. 10 and Aug. 25, 1931, p. 12.
76 Laski, *The Crisis and the Constitution: 1931 and After*, pp. 25 et seq.
77 The London *Times*, August 26, 1931, p. 12.

1931 in order to ask for a "doctor's mandate" to go on prescribing for the country's ills until the patient should be out of danger.[78]

From the foregoing paragraphs it may be gathered that since the end of the last century dissolutions of Parliament have generally been due to party decisions and reasons of party strategy. If the defeat of the Budget of the Liberal Government in the House of Lords in 1909 (which precipitated the dissolution in January, 1910) be taken as a party vote, since the Upper House was predominantly Conservative,[79] there were then distinctly five such cases. In 1900 and in January and November, 1910, Parliament was dissolved by the party in power despite the majority support in the House of Commons. Dissolution was resorted to in 1900 with the view of gaining a party advantage at the polls from victory on the battle fields; in January, 1910 in order to solve the deadlock between the Liberal majority in the House of Commons and the Conservative majority in the House of Lords on the matter of finance; and in December, 1910 for the purpose of securing a decision by the electorate of the issue of the relations between the two Houses, which a joint conference of the representatives of the two parties had failed to settle. The resignation in 1922 of the Lloyd George Government and the subsequent dissolution of Parliament were the result of a decision by the Conservative Party to withdraw its support from a Liberal Prime Minister; and the downfall in 1931 of the second Labour Government which necessitated dissolution of Parliament came after negotiations between the king and the party leaders and those between the Labour Prime Minister and leaders of Opposition parties.

It is evident from the examples just given that since 1900

---

[78] *Annual Register,* 1931, English History, pp. 78 *et seq.*
[79] *Cf.* Lowell, *Government of England,* vol. i, p. 409.

there has been an increased influence of party decisions and reasons of party strategy on the practice of dissolution, a development which it is plausible to associate with the growth of party organization during the same period. But at least two other factors also deserve consideration, *viz.*, the appearance of the theory of the mandate and the connection between the dissolution of Parliament and the returns of by-elections. This connection may be found to exist in two respects. In the first place, there are several instances where the defeat in the House of Commons, which led a government to dissolve Parliament, resulted from the government's majority having been gradually worn away by a series of unfavorable by-elections. There are, furthermore, at least two instances where such unfavorable by-elections were advanced as reasons why Parliament had been or ought to be dissolved.

Before 1868 by-elections had no bearing upon the existence of the government except in the years 1840 and 1841.[80] The Melbourne Government, which had secured a majority of forty at the polls in 1837, had its majority reduced to five on February 25, 1841 on the second reading of the Irish Registration Bill.[81] In that month Conservatives, in three by-elections, replaced Whigs; whereas in other single contests, although the Whigs were able to maintain their seats, the votes for the Conservatives showed increase over those at the last General Election. Two months later, the government sustained another defeat. " John Walter of *The Times* went down as Conservative candidate and carried Nottingham, which had been hitherto the seat of unsoiled Liberalism." So, when the Parliament was reassembled at

[80] In the thirty-six years before 1868 there were only four Parliaments (1837-41, 1847-52, 1852-57, 1859-65) in which Conservatives and Liberals were nearly equal in numerical strength. By-elections were of no great consequence in the dissolutions of 1852, 1857 and 1865. Their place in 1841 we discuss above.

[81] 56 *Hansard* (Commons) 3 s., 1020-1131.

the end of April after the March recess the government, on account of these losses at by-elections and the defection of the group of Whigs led by Lord Howick, was put into a minority of 11 on the Committee stage of the same bill. When, on May 7, the government minority on the Budget was increased to 36 the government decided to dissolve Parliament.[82]

Since the reform bill of 1867, greater importance should, however, be attached to by-elections than in the earlier period. The change on the political horizon was noticeable not only in the new leadership furnished by the two parties but also in the intensification of party strife in the rank and file of both parties due to the development of party organizations in local regions.[83] From that time on, the contests at by-elections naturally assumed greater practical significance, since they were waged more and more by the candidates chosen from the two big political camps rather than by people who cherished independent beliefs or who meant, if elected, to take independent action.[84] It may therefore be worth while to discuss in some detail the by-elections since then in order to see how they caused, or at least hastened, the dissolutions of Parliament.

To begin with, the majority of one hundred seats secured by Mr. Gladstone at the General Election of 1868[85] might have been large enough to maintain his government until the end of the legal term of Parliament, yet the government he

[82] Clark, *Peel and the Conservative Party*, pp. 464, et seq. Cf. *Letters of Queen Victoria, 1837–1861*, vol. i, pp. 353-354.

[83] Lowell, *The Government of England*, vol. i, pp. 480 et seq.

[84] Cf. the cases, as enumerated by Lowell (*ibid.*, vol. ii, p. 80), in which a majority of the party in power went into the lobby against the government whips and note his general remark that:

"During the middle period of the century it was not uncommon for a Cabinet to be saved from defeat at the hands of its own followers by the help of its opponents. Now such a thing has become extremely rare."

[85] *The Constitutional Year Book*, 1933, pp. 255-6.

formed was so much weakened, on account of the losses at by-elections which it sustained as well as from other causes, that he had to appeal to the country for support at the beginning of 1874. Since dissolution was suddenly resorted to by the Prime Minister, without the previous consent of the Cabinet, on grounds which might in a way be considered constitutionally dubious, perhaps it should be discussed here in considerable detail.

On March 11, 1873 the Gladstone Government was defeated on the second reading of the Irish University Bill by a majority of three (with 284 for and 287 against the government.) [86] As a result, Gladstone resigned and a constitutional crisis ensued. Finally, when it was clear that Disraeli would not take office without a dissolution, that neither Gladstone nor Disraeli would or could advise a dissolution and that there was no one else who could form a Cabinet, Gladstone had no alternative but to resume office.[87] As the head of a very much weakened government, he soon found himself confronted with further difficulties. "An inquiry into certain irregularities at the general post office led to the discovery that the sum of eight hundred thousand pounds had been detained on its way to the exchequer, and applied to the service of the telegraphs." Among the persons involved was Mr. Lowe, the Chancellor of the Exchequer. This "post office scandal" necessitated a reconstruction of the Cabinet by which the "resumption of the seals of the exchequer . . . was forced upon Mr. Gladstone by his colleagues." [88] The assumption by him of this office in addition to that of the first lord of the treasury then gave rise to the thorny question as to whether Gladstone had thereby vacated his seat at Greenwich, which he would not, it was

[86] 214 *Hansard* (Commons) 3 s., 1741-1868.

[87] *Cf.* Ponsonby, *Side Lights on Queen Victoria* (New York, 1930), p. 143.

[88] Morley, *Life of Gladstone*, vol. ii, pp. 460-463.

generally maintained, be able to hold in case of a fresh election.[89] Meanwhile, he was in active controversy with Mr. Cardwell, the Secretary for War, and Mr. Goschen, First Lord of the Admiralty, over the military and naval estimates for the year 1874-1875 which Mr. Gladstone considered excessive.[90] Furthermore, the Liberal government had been sustaining increasing losses at by-elections, and the seats lost to the Conservatives during the period of a little over five years amounted to twenty-four.[91] Of these losses, Gladstone himself said on April 24, 1874 in the new Parliament (Parliament of 1874-1880) : [92]

I conceived it was a peculiarity of which I knew no parallel within the Parliamentary experience of the present century . . . I have never known a Parliament . . . in which single elections

[89] The Earl of Selborne in his *Memorials* discussed this question at considerable length and then concluded that Gladstone had vacated his seat by accepting the office of the Chancellor of the Exchequer; that "a dissolution was the only escape" from the "formidable penalties" by the House of Commons; and that he had "never doubted that this was the determining cause of the dissolution of January, 1874." [*Part II, Personal and Political, 1865–1896* (London, 1898), vol. i, pp. 326-330.] To this, Lord Morley replied: "I can only say that in the mass of papers connected with the Greenwich seat and the dissolution, there is no single word in one of them associating in any way either topic with the other." *Op. cit.*, vol. ii, pp. 471-2.

[90] Elliot, *Life of Lord Goschen*, vol. i, pp. 140-141.

[91] *The Constitutional Year Book*, 1924, pp. 263-264.
The Ministerial gains and losses at the by-elections, 1868-1874:

	Losses	Gains
1869	4	2
1870	5	4
1871	6	
1872	7	
1873	7	
1874	1	
Totals	30	6

Net Loss (6 Years) 24 seats.

[92] 218 *Hansard* (Commons) 3 s., 1121-1122.

of themselves went so far towards establishing a presumption that the opinion of the country had changed with reference to the politics of those whom it desired to conduct public affairs as that of the last, and the consequence was that from time to time it was a matter of inquiry to us whether our position gave us the strength that was necessary to enable us to conduct with dignity and with credit the affairs of the country.

Under such circumstances, and especially because of the " unaccommodated difference " of opinion, to use Mr. Gladstone's phrase, with two of his principal colleagues as to the provision to be made for the army and navy in the estimates of 1874-1875,[93] Gladstone could pursue no other course than to advise for dissolution, as the alternative of resignation seemed to him to have been " cut off " since March, 1873.[94]

Between 1874 and 1931 there have been fifteen dissolutions. Except in 1880-1885, 1892-1895, 1900-1905 and 1918-1922, the returns of by-elections could not be said to have had much influence upon the existence of the Cabinet or Parliament. They did no more than serve as a barometer to indicate in what direction the political wind was blowing across the country. On five occasions—1874-1880,[95] 1886-1892, 1895-1900, 1906-1910, and 1924-1929—the majorities for the party in power were big enough to allow without

[93] Lord Morley's view (op. cit., vol. ii, pp. 478-487), concurred in by Elliot, the Biographer of Lord Goschen (op. cit., vol. i, p. 150), was that the dissolution of 1874 was primarily due to this " unaccommodated difference " of opinion in the Cabinet.

[94] Letters of Queen Victoria, 1862–1885, vol. ii, pp. 303-305.

[95] When Queen Victoria opened Parliament in February, 1880, it was uncertain whether its dissolution, inevitable in any case during the year (which was its seventh), would be decreed for the spring or the autumn. Encouraged by favorable by-elections at Liverpool and Southwark, ministers however decided to advise a dissolution at once. Cf. ibid., vol. iii, p. 61, Introductory Notes to Chapter II, and Monypenny and Buckle, Life of Disraeli, vol. vi, pp. 512-513.

embarrassment the occasional swearing-in of members of the Opposition as a result of by-elections. The dissolution at the end of each period could hardly be attributed to the cumulative unfavorable returns of single elections. During four other periods—1885-1886, January-November, 1910, 1922-1923 and January-October, 1924—the existence of Parliament was too short to have been threatened by adverse returns of by-elections. Finally, in 1910-1918 and 1929-1931 when the Liberal and Labour governments depended largely upon the support of the Irish Nationalists and Liberals respectively for their majorities, the loss at by-elections, considerable in each case, might have been a factor in causing resignation or dissolution. But in reality the dissolutions of 1918 and 1931, resorted to during periods of national crisis, had little or no connection with by-elections.[96]

Now, when we turn to the period of 1880-1885 we notice that during its six years in office the Gladstone Government had been undergoing constant disapproval at by-elections, and that the net loss at the end of the administration amounted to nineteen seats. Had there not been such a

[96]

	Result of General Election					Net Ministerial Loss at by-elections
1874	C. 352	L.......... 242	N... 58			
1874–1880						5
1886	C. 316	L. U........ 78	G. L. 191	N..... 85		
1886–1892						20
1895	C. 341	L. U........ 70	G. L. 177	N..... 82		
1895–1900						11
1906	C. 134	L. U........ 23	L... 376	Lab... 54	N. 83	
1906–1910						15
1910(Dec.)	C. 240	L. U........ 34	L... 270	Lab... 42	N. 84	
1910–1918						15
1924	C. 412	Constitutional 7	L... 40	Soc.. 151	Ind. 5	
1924–1929						15
1929	C. 260	L.......... 59	Soc.. 288	Others 8		
1929–1931						3

The Constitutional Year Book, 1924, pp. 263-4; 1933, pp. 255-6. The Liberal Year Book, 1930, p. 181; 1932, p. 186.

heavy loss, the defeat of the government on the Budget
(which led to the resignation of Mr. Gladstone and the dissolution of Parliament by Lord Salisbury shortly afterwards)
by a majority of only twelve might have been averted despite
the alliance of Tories and Irish and the breach between the
Whigs and Radicals.[97]

What was true in 1885 regarding the Gladstone Government was also true ten years later of another Liberal government which had been formed by Lord Rosebery. In 1892,
the Gladstone Liberals, who did not by themselves constitute
a clear majority in the new House of Commons, were put in
office by a majority of forty on the vote on the Amendment
to the Address. They had the support of the eighty-one
Nationalists.[98] The constant ministerial loss at by-elections
in the three succeeding years,[99] however, coupled with the

[97] The result of the General Election of 1880: C., 238; L., 349; N., 95.
The Ministerial gains and losses at the by-elections, 1880-1885:

	Losses	Gains
1880	8	1
1881	6	1
1882	1	1
1883	4	2
1884	4	
1885	2	1
Totals	25	6

Net Loss (6 years) 19 seats. *The Constitutional Year Book*, 1924, pp.
263-4; 1933, pp. 255-6.

[98] 7 *Hansard* (Commons) 4 s., 433-446; 7 *Hansard* (Lords) 4 s., 447;
Letters of Queen Victoria, 1886-1901, vol. ii, p. 140.

[99] The result of the General Election of 1892: C., 268; L. U., 47; G. L.,
274 and N., 81.
The Ministerial gains and losses at the by-elections, 1892-1895:

	Losses	Gains
1893	4	3
1894	2	
1895	3	1
Totals	9	4

Net Loss (3 years) 5 seats. *The Constitutional Year Book*, 1924, pp.

withdrawal of support by the Parnellite Irish Nationalists, had, by the middle of 1895 made the position of the government extremely precarious. The government, as we have said, was finally turned into a minority of seven votes on a " snap" division. Lord Rosebery resigned and his successor, Lord Salisbury, dissolved Parliament almost at once.

The Conservative Government, which had won renewed support at the General Election of 1900, had since 1903 faced not only the difficulty of holding itself together on the fiscal issue but also the misfortune of constantly losing by-elections.[100] By February, 1905 the loss sustained by the government at by-elections proved to be so great that Sir H. Campbell-Bannerman, the leader of the Opposition, raised the question whether the government should cling to office when the feeling of the country was turning against it.[101] After the government was actually defeated on July 20 of the same year by a vote of 199 to 196 in the House of Commons on the Civil Services and Revenue Departments Estimates,[102] a similar debate ensued on July 24. To sup-

263-4; 1933, pp. 255-6. *Cf.* Whates, *The Third Salisbury Administration, 1895–1900*, pp. 1-2; Griffith-Boscawen, *Fourteen Years in Parliament*, pp. 69-74.

[100] The result of the General Election of 1900: C., 334; L. U., 68; L., 186 and N., 82.

The Ministerial gains and losses at the by-elections, 1900-1905:

	Losses	Gains
1901	1	1
1902	3	1
1903	5	
1904	7	
1905	7	
Totals	23	2

Net loss (5½ years) 21 seats. *The Constitutional Year Book*, 1924, pp. 263-4; 1933, pp. 225-6.

[101] 141 *Hansard* (Commons) 4 s., 123 *et seq.*

[102] 149 *Hansard* (Commons) 4 s., 1409-1490.

port their respective positions both the Prime Minister and the Leader of the Opposition cited what Gladstone had said in 1874 in regard to the dissolution of that year. The position of Mr. Balfour, as he reiterated it on August 19, was that: [103]

There is one plain test whether the Government can carry on the business of the country, and that plain test is whether the House of Commons supports them. I do not believe any other plain test can be provided. Every other test is open to doubt, is open to qualification. Those who are defeated at by-elections are always rich in explanations why that particular disaster should have happened. The conditions under which a by-election is taken are very different from those which obtain at a general election, and necessarily different, and, if the Prime Minister or his Government has to undertake the duty not merely of gauging the opinion of the House of Commons, not merely, to the best of his ability, of carrying on by the help of that House of Commons the general policy of the country at home and abroad, but has to make the very existence of his Government depend on what may be a temporary wave of popular feeling, it seems that you reduce the British constitution to an absurdity . . . to say that whenever by-elections are going against you, you are therefore, and for that reason alone, immediately to dissolve the House and seek the opinion of the country is not only not in conformity with the essential principles of the British Constitution, but . . . it would be the greatest blow that could be dealt against free representative institutions, because you would emphasise the essential weakness, perhaps the only weakness, of free institutions—namely, that they are subject, however you arrange them, to violent flows backwards and forwards of popular opinion.

On the other hand, Sir H. Campbell-Bannerman maintained that: [104]

[103] 151 *Hansard* (Commons) 4 s., 975-978.
[104] 150 *Hansard* (Commons) 4 s., 70-75.

. . . it is common for us to say, and it is true constitutionally, that the Minister of the Crown in this country is selected and appointed because he is the man who commands a majority in the House of Commons. But what does that mean? It means that the command of the majority of the House represents the feeling of the country. The moment the House of Commons get out of touch and harmony with the country then that plea for retaining office dissolves. . . .

Whatever view the Prime Minister took as regards the relation between the retention of office and loss in by-elections, the Balfour Government, having failed in a final effort to secure the united support of the Unionist Party, resigned at the end of 1905,[105] and thus paved the way for the dissolution by the Liberal Government which succeeded it.

The most recent case in which the dissolution of Parliament might be attributed partly to the adverse returns of by-elections was that of the downfall of the Coalition Government in 1922. As far back as December, 1921, the Unionist Central Office informed Mr. Austen Chamberlain of the difficulties that were arising in the constituencies—as phrased by Sir George Younger, the Chairman of the National Unionist Association, " not so much in the House of Com-

---

[105] A. L. Lowell noted in his book *The Government of England* (vol. i, pp. 440-441), that the claim was reiterated by the Opposition during the latter part of Mr. Balfour's administration that " although supported by a majority in the House of Commons, he ought to resign, because a long series of by-elections had shown that he had lost the confidence of the country. His retention of office under those conditions was said to be contrary to the spirit of the Constitution; and Mr. Balfour's resignation late in 1905, when Parliament was not in session, involved an acknowledgement, if not of the necessity, at least of the propriety, of withdrawing from office in such a case. Former cabinets have sometimes broken up on account of dissensions among their members, or the impossibility of maintaining an efficient government; but there has been no previous instance of a cabinet, supported by a majority in Parliament, which has resigned apparently in consequence of a change of popular sentiment."

mons as in the constituencies." [106] Later on, as the demand by the Conservatives for independence of the coalition gained momentum, the dissatisfaction in the constituencies steadily grew. The movement for independence "derived much encouragement from the declaration of the result of a by-election at Newport, where a Conservative was elected by a majority of 2,090 for a seat that had been won by a Coalition-Liberal by a large majority in 1918," [107] and finally culminated in the decision at the Carlton Club which precipitated the resignation of the Coalition Government and the subsequent dissolution of Parliament.

We have now considered the following reasons for dissolution: the demise of the Crown, near-efflux of the legal term, dismissal by the sovereign, dispute between the two Houses, party decisions and reasons of party strategy, adverse votes in the House of Commons, minority government appealing to the country for support on assuming office, and loss of by-elections. Among these, the last three are what Sir William Anson called the "usual grounds" for dissolution. "They represent different forms of the same proposition, namely, that a dissolution is rightly demanded if there is

[106] *Gleanings and Memoranda,* vol. 56 (1922), pp. 509-11, as cited by Sait and Barrows, *British Politics in Transition,* pp. 214-17.

The *Constitutional Year Book,* 1924, pp. 263-4; 1933, 255-6; The result of the General Election of 1918: Co. U., 334; Col. L., 136; Co. Lab., 13; U., 50; L., 29; Lab., 59; Nat., 7; S. F., 73; and Others, 6.

The Ministerial gains and losses at the by-elections, 1918-1922:

	Losses	Gains
1919	6	
1920	4	
1921	7	1
1922	6	1
Totals	23	2

Net loss (4 years) 21 seats.

[107] *Annual Register,* 1922, English History, p. 113.

reason to suppose that the House of Commons and the majority of the electorate are at variance." On the other hand, the theory of "the mandate," if we mean by it that "no novel or important legislative measure ought to be introduced in Parliament unless it has been brought prominently to the notice of the constituencies at a previous general election," was considered to be one of the "doubtful cases." [108] Such a theory, if so constantly applied as to constitute an important element in the British political system, would not only impair the principles of Parliamentary sovereignty and representative government but also nullify the principle of Cabinet responsibility to the House of Commons by creating two separate centres of authority in the Constitution—the Parliament and the plebiscite. The violation of those established principles of the Constitution might be avoided through the employment of the argument that the device of the referendum is adopted by a leader in difficulties "as a way of escape from the embarrassments of the moment." [109] Nevertheless, recent practice clearly indicates that such an argument is not exactly applicable in every case where Parliament has been dissolved by the government for the purpose of seeking a mandate from the electorate.

The "tendency to ask for a mandate on a single, and as far as possible, a simple issue grows with the growth of 'democracy' and with the extension of the suffrage." [110]

[108] Anson, *The Law and Custom of the Constitution*, vol. i, pp. 306-8.

The other doubtful case Sir William Anson mentioned is the necessity of appealing to the country as soon as possible after a change in electoral conditions, as in 1832, in 1867-8, in 1884-1885 and in 1918. *Cf.* Todd, *On Parliamentary Government in England*, vol. i, p. 255; The Earl of Oxford and Asquith, *Fifty Years of British Parliament*, vol. ii, p. 218, and Churchill, *The World Crisis, the Aftermath*, pp. 40-41.

[109] *Cf.* Samuel, "The Device of the Referendum," *The Nation and Athenæum*, vol. 46, pp. 791-2, March 15, 1930.

[110] J. A. R. Marriott, in his three articles under the title "The Answer of Demos" (*Fortnightly Review*, vol. 121, pp. 105-117, January, 1924; vol.

Possibly with the exception of 1857, no issue was sufficiently clear in any of the General Elections before 1867.[111] In 1857 the constituencies of the country were asked to judge between the Palmerston Government and " any other administration which might be formed." [112] Since the reform of 1867, however, elections have often been fought on single issues. In 1868 the question was that of the Irish Church.[113] The 1886 election, coming only one year and a half after further extension of the suffrage, turned on Irish Home Rule,[114] and that of 1895, on the same issue together with the question of deprivation of the legislative power of the House of Lords.[115] It should be remarked, however, that the opinion of the country was taken in 1868 on the Irish Church and in 1886 on Irish Home Rule after the Disraeli and Gladstone Governments had been defeated in the House of Commons on those issues and a vote of support from the electorate was asked for in 1857 after the Palmerston Government had been censured by the House of Commons on the China War. As for Irish Home Rule in 1895, that was an issue on which the Conservative Government, then in a minority, and the majority of the representatives of the people were at vari-

132, pp. 10-18, July, 1929 and vol. 136, pp. 681-2, December, 1931), described very briefly the theory of " the mandate" as implied in political battles at General Elections from 1832 to 1931.

[111] The predominant issue at the General Elections of 1841 and 1852 was Free Trade versus Protection. For further details see *Annual Register*, 1841, History of Europe, pp. 143-5; 1852, History of England, p. 124.

[112] *Letters of Queen Victoria, 1837–1861*, vol. iii, pp. 290-291; 144 *Hansard* (Lords) 3 s., 1885-1886; 144 *Hansard* (Commons) 3 s., 1894-1897.

[113] *Letters of Queen Victoria, 1862–1885*, vol. i, pp. 523-526; 191 *Hansard* (Commons) 3 s., 1694-1708.

[114] *Letters of Queen Victoria, 1886–1901*, vol. i, pp. 143-4; 307 *Hansard* (Lords) 3 s., 276-8.

[115] *Annual Register*, 1895, English History, pp. 148-152.

ance.[116] Since the dissolutions on all those occasions were demanded chiefly because of the disagreement between the government and the House of Commons and because of the supposition by the government that the House of Commons did not correctly represent the opinion of the country, they should be considered to have been resorted to on what Anson called " the usual grounds," although the idea of asking for a mandate was implied in each case.

There have been ten dissolutions since 1895. If we leave those in 1906, 1924 and 1929 out of account,[117] we find the prevailing phenomenon, common to them all, that the appeal to the country was made in order to secure a mandate in dealing with some special matter in hand, despite the fact that the government still had a majority and had not suffered decisive defeat in the House of Commons. What was considered by Anson in 1909 to be " doubtful " ground was actually the basis of the dissolutions of January and November, 1910 and 1923. For in those elections the people were asked to pass judgment respectively

(1) upon the Asquith Government's Finance Bill embodying the proposals for a reassessment of land values, taxation of unearned increment, and, in general, heavier impositions upon wealth;

---

[116] The Liberal Government's Irish Home Rule Bill was passed on its third reading on September 1, 1893, in the House of Commons by a vote of 301 against 267 [16 *Hansard* (Commons) 4 s., 1839]; but it was rejected by a vote of 419 against 41 a week later on its second reading in the House of Lords. 17 *Hansard* (Lords) 4 s., 649.

[117] Parliament was dissolved in 1906 by the Campbell-Bannerman Government, then a minority government, on its assumption of office, and in 1924 by the MacDonald Government after it had been defeated on the Campbell case. In 1918 and 1929 Parliament came to an end as its legal duration had expired; yet in 1918 the Coalition Government under Lloyd George definitely appealed for authority in carrying on the peace negotiations and national reconstruction immediately following the Armistice.

(2) upon its resolutions regulating the relations between the two Houses and the duration of the House of Commons and (3) upon Mr. Baldwin's idea of a protective tariff.

In 1900, 1918, 1922 and 1931 Parliament was brought to an end not so much as " a way of escape from the embarrassments of the moment " but as a plea for renewed confidence from the electorate during national crises. For instance, one of the reasons why Parliament was dissolved in 1900, as Lord Salisbury reported to Queen Victoria, was that the Conservative Government would " act with much more confidence and effect " if they were " fully acquainted with the views of the electors " regarding the South African War, and were " assured of their support." [118] In 1918 the appeal of the Coalition was for full authority to negotiate peace and carry on national reconstruction.[119] Four years later renewed confidence was asked for by the new Conservative Government and a vote of approval was sought for the return of " the normal procedure which existed before the War." [120] And, finally, the National Government's appeal in 1931 was for a free hand to deal with the economic emergency.[121]

The government's recent practice of dissolving Parliament in order to obtain a mandate on a definite issue necessarily gives rise to the question whether Parliament is morally restrained from dealing with questions that have not been laid before the people at the preceding General Election. The idea that Parliament is so restrained would, as A. L. Lowell remarked in 1908, " formerly have been regarded as a dangerous political heresy." " Yet," he added, " during the recent agitation (in 1903-1906) in regard to fiscal policy,

[118] *Letters of Queen Victoria, 1886–1901,* vol. iii, p. 586.

[119] The London *Times,* November 18, 1918, p. 9, Prime Minister Lloyd George's Address.

[120] *Ibid.,* October 27, 1922, p. 12, Prime Minister Bonar Law's Address.

[121] *Ibid.,* October 8, 1931, p. 10, Prime Minister MacDonald's Address.

Mr. Balfour, while repudiating the suggestion that the existing Parliament, having been elected on the single issue of the South African War, ought to be dissolved when peace was made, refused to grant time for a debate for free food, on the ground that it would be constitutionally improper for Parliament to act on the question until it had been submitted to the people at a general election, and that it would be unwise for the House to discuss a subject on which it could not act." [122] Now, we may add that in 1923 Mr. Baldwin, who intended to use protective tariff as a means of relieving unemployment, was morally hampered by Mr. Bonar Law's pledge one year before that the Conservative proposals for dealing with the unemployment situation were "to reduce expenditure to the lowest attainable level" and to stimulate "further development of trade with oversea countries, and especially of trade within the British Empire." [128] He therefore appealed to the country to "release" him from the pledge and give him the mandate he asked for.[124] In general, the position taken by the British statesmen since the beginning of the present century as regards the theory of the mandate has been that, while maintaining an unyielding attitude in regard to the legal omnipotence of Parliament, they were not unaware of the constitutional propriety and practical expediency of asking for fresh authority in dealing with some novel and important measure or some unusual situation.

Of the twenty-six dissolutions which have been dealt with

[122] Lowell, *The Government of England*, vol. i, p. 440 and *cf.*:
    113 *Hansard* (Commons) 4 s., 49-50.
    131 *Hansard* (Commons) 4 s., 290.
    132 *Hansard* (Commons) 4 s., 1013-1015.
    141 *Hansard* (Commons) 4 s., 163-4.
    145 *Hansard* (Commons) 4 s., 627.
    146 *Hansard* (Commons) 4 s., 496, 987-989.

[128] The London *Times*, October 27, 1922, p. 12, Prime Minister Bonar Law's Address.

[124] 168 *H. C. Deb.* 5 s., 39-40.

in this chapter seven (1837, 1847, 1865, 1880, 1892, 1918, 1919) were the result mainly of legal stipulations. The other nineteen are to be accounted for by a number of reasons. The least important of these has been action by the sovereign which can be used to explain only the dissolution of 1834. So, too, only once (January, 1910) was a dispute between the two Houses a potent element in the decision to go to the people. By-election returns, on the other hand, while of no consequence before 1868 are found to influence a government's line of action on several occasions since then.

About the remaining three reasons for dissolution certain significant conclusions can be reached. It seems rather important, in the first place, that of the nineteen dissolutions resulting from the exercise of the royal prerogative only six (1841, 1857, 1859, 1868, 1886, 1924) were the direct result and only three (1852, 1885, 1895) the indirect result of government defeats in the House of Commons. Even more significantly only one of the nine cases just alluded to occurred after 1895. Moreover, in the last three (1852, 1885, 1895) of the above dissolutions, as in certain others (1834, 1905) with which we are not directly concerned at this point, an important element in the decision to advise dissolution seems to have been the fact that the government of the day was in a minority from its inception, had only recently assumed office, and had, therefore, practically no choice but to go to the country immediately or after a very short delay.

A second point that should receive emphasis here is the changing character of the connection between party politics and dissolution. We have already shown that the votes in the House of Commons that led, directly or indirectly, to dissolution in nine instances were linked with various shifts in party alignments or with the defection of certain groups from their former party allegiance. But there was always a vote in the House of Commons, a government defeat at the hands of the elected representatives, as well as the manoeuvres of party. Not until 1900 do party decisions taken outside the House of Commons, or reasons of party strategy alone, become a direct cause of dissolution. But since 1900 this factor had been present in no fewer than four cases (1900, November, 1910, 1922, 1931).

Finally, among significant developments must be mentioned the rise of the theory of mandate, so well defined by Anson. Here, too, a new period seems to have opened about 1900. Prior to that date there were some elections (1857, 1868, 1886, 1895) in which were present traces of the idea of mandate, at least to the extent that the government of the day sought "a refreshment of its authority," to use a phrase of Professor Laski,[125] mainly on one issue. But our examination of elections since 1900 shows that the desire to have direct authority from the people to deal with specific matters has become a more important factor in the use of the power of dissolution than was ever the case in the nineteenth century.

[125] Laski, *The Crisis and the Constitution: 1931 and After*, p. 18.

CHAPTER IV

How Parliaments Were Dissolved

The power of dissolution, as we have said, is a royal prerogative exercised by the sovereign but only on the advice and at the request of his ministers. As soon as the ministers of the Crown have advised a dissolution and the sovereign has given his sanction to such an act, the Parliament may be regarded as having been dissolved, subject to the disposition of certain " necessary business " [1] and resort to certain formal dissolution procedure. According to modern constitutional practice, it is not necessary for the ministers under the rules of Parliamentary responsibility even to announce dissolution in Parliament before the issuance of the Royal Proclamation. Among the twenty-six dissolutions since the passing of the Reform Bill in 1832, eight—1832, 1834, 1847, 1874, 1900, 1906, 1918 and 1922—were not announced at all.[2] That of 1837 was announced through a Message from

[1] Alpheus Todd said: " By necessary business is to be understood such measures as are imperatively required for the public service, or as may be proceeded upon by common consent." Of the measures that may be proceeded upon by common consent, he remarked: " In 1868 . . . this wholesome constitutional rule (the rule, when Parliament is about to be dissolved, to restrict the grant of supplies to an amount sufficient to defray the indispensable requirements of the public service, until the new Parliament can be assembled) was departed from by common consent, for reasons of public convenience, and the supplies were voted for the whole fiscal year (ending March 31, 1869) although a dissolution of Parliament was agreed upon early in June. The Prorogation took place on July 31, the dissolution in November, and the new Parliament met on December 10, 1868." *On Parliamentary Government in England,* vol. ii, pp. 503-504.

[2] On May 28, 1900, Mr. Labouchere, M.P. for Northampton, asked the government, in the House of Commons, when the dissolution was going

the Queen read, not by the ministers, but by the Lord Chancellor and the Speaker in the House of Lords and the House of Commons respectively.[3] Those in 1852,[4] 1892,[5] and 1929[6] were made known by the spokesmen of the existing governments through answers to questions raised in the House of Commons. In the remaining fourteen cases, dissolution was announced through ministerial statements, either in the House of Commons,[7] or in the House of Lords,[8] or in both Houses simultaneously.[9]

to take place, but the government did not even reply. 83 *Hansard* (Commons) 4 s., 1570-1572.

On November 7, 1918, when the question of dissolution was raised in the House of Commons in connection with the debate on the Parliament adjournment motion introduced by Mr. Dillon, Mr. Bonar Law, the Chancellor of the Exchequer, explicitly manifested his inability to make any statement on the matter at all. He said: " The only statement I hope to make today was when the Session would end and what business would be taken before that date." 110 *H. C. Deb.* 5 s., 2411 *et seq.*

[3] 38 *Hansard* (Lords) 3 s., 1546-1554; 38 *Hansard* (Commons) 3 s., 1554-1564.

[4] 119 *Hansard* (Commons) 3 s., 1299-1302.

[5] 5 *Hansard* (Commons) 4 s., 1470-1472.

[6] 227 *H. C. Deb.* 5 s., 880-882.

[7] June 7, 1841, 58 *Hansard* (Commons) 3 s., 1260-1266; December 2, 1909, 13 *H. C. Deb.* 5 s., 550; November 13, 1923, 168 *H. C. Deb.* 5 s., 39-40.

[8] In 1885 and 1895 dissolution was announced in the House of Lords only by the Prime Minister who happened to be a member of that House. The dates when Lord Salisbury made his statements (on assumption of office) were as follows: June 25, 1885, 298 *Hansard* (Lords) 3 s., 1631-1636; June 27, 1895, 35 *Hansard* (Lords) 4 s., 24-25.

[9] March 5, 1857, 144 *Hansard* (Lords) 3 s., 1885-1886; 144 *Hansard* (Commons) 3 s., 1894-1897.

April 4, 1859, 153 *Hansard* (Lords) 3 s., 1264-1291; 153 *Hansard* (Commons) 3 s., 1301-1307.

June 27, 1865, 180 *Hansard* (Lords) 3 s., 850-851; 180 *Hansard* (Commons) 3 s., 914.

May 4, 1868, 191 *Hansard* (Lords) 3 s., 1686; 191 *Hansard* (Commons) 3 s., 1694-1708.

After a dissolution has been announced, the government usually drops Public Bills of a contentious character and then gives a Notice of Motion that uncontested Public Bills and Business of Supply—Army and Navy Estimates and Account for the Civil Services—shall have precedence. The House of Commons has to proceed upon business transmitted from the House of Lords. Proceedings in pursuance of an Act of Parliament requiring any Order, Rule, or Regulation to be laid before the House of Commons are usually taken up immediately after government business, in order to give private interests which may be affected power to appeal. The time for that, as Mr. Balfour remarked on June 17, 1892 in the House of Commons, " cannot be shortened without violating all the tenets of public equity, which both Houses have invariably observed." [10] With respect to private business with which the government does not intend to deal, it is requisite, in conformity with precedent, to pass a Resolution for the purpose of taking up Private Bills in the new Parliament at the point which the previous Parliament may have reached in its discussion of such bills.[11] No session in the House of Commons may be brought to a close until the business of the House of Lords has also been terminated; in general it takes about two weeks, after the announcement

March 8, 1880, 251 *Hansard* (Lords) 3 s., 547; 251 *Hansard* (Commons) 3 s., 557-560.

June 10, 1886, 306 *Hansard* (Lords) 3 s., 1254; 306 *Hansard* (Commons) 3 s., 1304-1306.

November 18, 1910, 6 *H. L. Deb.* 5 s., 760-766; 20 *H. C. Deb.* 5 s., 82-87.

October 9, 1924, 59 *H. L. Deb.* 5 s., 667; 177 *H. C. Deb.* 5 s., 731.

October 6, 1931, 82 *H. L. Deb.* 5 s., 266-267; 257 *H. C. Deb.* 5 s., 980-981.

[10] 5 *Hansard* (Commons) 4 s., 1470-2.

[11] 306 *Hansard* (Commons) 3 s., 1304-6.

of dissolution, for the Houses of Parliament to dispose of their remaining business.[12]

With regard to the procedure by which Parliament is dissolved, it may be said at the outset that, in case of the expiration of the term, dissolution may technically come about without the exercise of the royal prerogative. But, as we have said,[13] since no Parliament has been allowed to continue for its full term, dissolution has always been brought about by the sovereign on the advice of his ministers. When the Crown exercises its prerogative, the usual practice, if Parliament is in session, is for the sovereign to hold two Councils —one for proroguing Parliament and another for dissolving it—a procedure Sir Almeric Fitzroy, as Clerk of the Council,

[12] By leaving out of account the eight dissolutions which were not announced in Parliament before the Royal Proclamations were issued—as well as those in 1852, 1868 and 1885 which could take place only after the lapse of a stated length of time because of unusual circumstances *—we can calculate the average time needed for disposal of business in Parliament after dissolution had been announced. According to the following table, it is about fourteen days:

Dissolution Announced		Parliament Dissolved		Interval Between
June	22, 1837	July	17, 1837	25 days
June	7, 1841	June	23, 1841	16 "
March	5, 1857	March	21, 1857	16 "
April	4, 1859	April	23, 1859	19 "
June	27, 1865	July	6, 1865	9 "
March	8, 1880	March	24, 1880	16 "
June	10, 1886	June	26, 1886	16 "
June	17, 1892	June	28, 1892	11 "
June	27, 1895	July	8, 1895	11 "
December	2, 1909	January	10, 1910	19 "
November	18, 1910	November	28, 1910	10 "
November	13, 1923	November	16, 1923	3 "
October	9, 1924	October	9, 1924	
April	24, 1929	May	10, 1929	16 "
October	4, 1931	October	7, 1931	3 "

* On the dissolution of 1852 see Morley, *Life of Gladstone*, vol. i, pp. 424-5. The delay in the dissolutions of 1868 and 1885 was caused by the necessity of registering new voters after the Reforms of 1867 and 1884.

[13] Cf. *supra*, p. 16, fn. 14.

"had great difficulty in making ministers understand."[14]
Each of the Councils so held, while in theory comprising the
whole body of the Privy Councillors, represents practically
only the Cabinet. It is attended in person by the sovereign,
who is never present at ordinary meetings of the Cabinet or
the Privy Council,[15] and is usually composed of four ministers including the Lord President whose place, during his
absence, is taken by the Lord Chancellor.[16] In these two
Councils, two separate Acts of State are arranged—an Order
proroguing Parliament and a Proclamation dissolving it;
but the latter instrument has to follow the formal prorogation
of Parliament in the House of Lords.[17] Of the twenty-six
dissolutions under discussion, eighteen took place when Parliament was in session,[18] while on the other eight occasions,

[14] Fitzroy, *Memoirs,* vol. ii, p. 424.

[15] MacDonagh, *The Book of Parliament* (London, 1897), pp. 428-429.

[16] Fitzroy, *op. cit.,* vol. ii, pp. 425-6; 687.

[17] *Ibid.,* vol. ii, p. 424.

[18] Excluding the case of 1922, which will be dealt with in the text,
the seventeen prorogations at the time of dissolution were as follows:

July	17, 1837	38 *Hansard* (Lords) 3 s.,	1919-1922
June	22, 1841	58 *Hansard* (Lords) 3 s.,	1594-1596
July	23, 1847	94 *Hansard* (Lords) 3 s.,	686-691
July	1, 1852	122 *Hansard* (Lords) 3 s.,	1424-1429
March	21, 1857	144 *Hansard* (Lords) 3 s.,	2476-2478
April	19, 1859	153 *Hansard* (Lords) 3 s.,	1898-1899
July	6, 1865	180 *Hansard* (Lords) 3 s.,	1178-1184
March	24, 1880	251 *Hansard* (Lords) 3 s.,	1268-1271
June	25, 1886	307 *Hansard* (Lords) 3 s.,	276-278
June	28, 1892	5 *Hansard* (Lords) 4 s.,	1933-1935
July	6, 1895	35 *Hansard* (Lords) 4 s.,	288-91
November	28, 1910	6 *H. L. Deb.* 5 s.,	1013-16
November	21, 1918	32 *H. L. Deb.* 5 s.,	371-4
November	16, 1923	55 *H. L. Deb.* 5 s.,	39-42
October	9, 1924	59 *H. L. Deb.* 5 s.,	684-8
May	10, 1929	74 *H. L. Deb.* 5 s.,	518-26
October	7, 1931	82 *H. L. Deb.* 5 s.,	300-2

dissolution was proclaimed after Parliament had been prorogued.[19] For dissolutions when Parliament stands prorogued, a royal proclamation has been sufficient. In such cases, only one Council has to be held—the Council for Dissolution.[20]

Except for prorogation of Parliament during recess, which has since 1867 been done merely by a royal proclamation issued by the sovereign " by and with the advice of Our Privy Council,"[21] the normal practice in closing a session of

[19]

Prorogation	*Dissolution*	
August 16, 1832		14 *Hansard* (Lords) 3 s., 1412-16
	December 3, 1832	*Journals of H. L.*, vol. 64, p. 467
August 15, 1834		25 *Hansard* (Lords) 3 s., 1265-69
	December 29, 1834	*Journals of H. L.*, vol. 66, p. 1000
July 31, 1868		193 *Hansard* (Lords) 3 s., 1937-40
	November 11, 1868	*Journals of H. L.*, vol. 100, p. 503
August 5, 1873		217 *Hansard* (Lords) 3 s., 1555-59
	January 26, 1874	*Journals of H. L.*, vol. 105, p. 743
August 14, 1885		301 *Hansard* (Lords) 3 s., 30-34
	November 18, 1885	*Journals of H. L.*, vol. 117, p. 474
August 8, 1900		87 *Hansard* (Lords) 4 s., 965-9
	September 17, 1900	*Journals of H. C.*, vol. 155, p. 404
August 11, 1905		151 *Hansard* (Lords) 4 s., 989-993
	January 8, 1906	*Journals of H. C.*, vol. 161, p. 2
December 3, 1909		4 *H. L. Deb.* 5 s., 1412-16
	January 10, 1910	*Journals of H. C.*, vol. 165, p. 2

[20] Fitzroy, *op. cit.*, vol. i, pp. 278, 392.

[21] " In former days if a prorogation affected a newly elected Parliament, or one which had been already prorogued to a certain day, it was necessary that Parliament should hold a formal meeting on the day originally fixed and that the further prorogation should be announced by a special writ, read by the Lord Chancellor in the House of Lords to the Peers and the Commons at the Lords' bar or that it should be done by a Commission of five Lords." (*Cf.* Redlich, *The Procedure of the House of Commons,* vol. ii, p. 66.) Since the act of 1867, entitled " an Act to Simplify the Forms of Prorogation during the Recess of Parliament ", a royal proclamation, " without any subsequent issue of a writ or writs patent or commission under the Great Seal of the United Kingdom," has been sufficient in such cases. For the closing of a

Parliament is through a formal prorogation in the House of Lords. The exercise of this prerogative may be carried out by the sovereign in person or, if not in person, by Royal Commission. In practice, however, Parliament has not been prorogued by the sovereign in person since August 12, 1854.[22] Because of the fact that the Parliament of 1918-1922 was dissolved during its adjournment simply through a royal proclamation without the formal process of prorogation in the House of Lords,[28] there were really only twenty-five prorogations immediately preceding the royal proclamation for dissolution. Of these, six—1832, 1834, 1837, 1841, 1847 and 1852—which took place before 1854 were attended by the sovereign in person, while the other nineteen—those taking place since 1854—were brought about by Royal Commission.[24]

With respect to the ceremony itself it may be briefly stated that shortly after two o'clock on the day fixed for proroguing Parliament the sovereign wearing his Crown went in state to the House of Lords and there took his seat on the Throne. Or, in case of prorogation by Commission, the Lords Com-

session, now as of old, prorogation must be brought about through solemn announcement in the House of Lords (30 & 31 Vict., c. 81).

For an example of a Royal Proclamation for Prorogation, see *Journals of H. L.* (1867), vol. 99, p. 629.

[22] *Journals of H. L.* (1854), vol. 86, p. 521. *Cf.* further *Journals of H. L.*, Index:

[23] *Journals of H. L.* (1922), vol. 154, p. 383.

[24] For reference, see *supra*, pp. 115, 116, footnotes 18 and 19.

missioners—five in number, of whom the Lord Chancellor is always one—would go to the House of Lords where they would sit in their scarlet robes and ermine on a bench between the Throne and the Woolsack. The Gentlemen Usher of the Black Rod was commanded to signify to the Speaker and members of the House of Commons that " it is His (or Her) Majesty's Pleasure that They attend Him (or Her) immediately in this House," or, in case of prorogation by Commission, " The Lords Commissioners desire their immediate attendance in this House, to hear the Commission read." The Speaker and Commons thus summoned would be at the bar of the House of Lords within five minutes. In former days, it was customary for the Speaker to address the sovereign, reviewing for him the labours of the session in the House of Commons and praying him to assent to the Bill of Supply for the service for the current year. But, as the sovereign has, since August 12, 1854, abstained from attending the prorogation in person, the Speaker's practice of addressing the " most Gracious Sovereign " has also fallen into desuetude. In the days when it was the custom of the sovereign to prorogue Parliament in person, the Speaker, after his speech, delivered the Money Bill to the Clerk, who brought it to the Table, where the Clerk of the Crown read its title together with those of other Bills to be passed. To these Bills the royal assent was pronounced by the Clerk Assistant. In case of prorogation by Commission it was necessary, before the pronouncement of the royal assent, for the Lord Chancellor first to announce to the House the formation of a Commission to give the royal assent to diverse acts agreed upon by both Houses of Parliament, then to direct the clerk to read the Commission [25] and finally to declare and notify to the Lords and Commons that " His (or

[25] For an example, see *Journals of H.L.* (1930-1931), vol. 163, pp. 379-80.

Her) Majesty hath given His (or Her) Royal Assent to the several Acts."

The royal assent having been given to various bills, the sovereign, or the Lord Chancellor, in pursuance of the sovereign's commands to the Lord Commissioners, delivered "His (or Her) Majesty's Most Gracious Speech." It usually contained congratulations to the Lords and Commons on the valuable additions to the Statute Book which their labours during the session had produced and also, in a separate paragraph, thanks for the supplies granted by the Commons, sometimes coupled with a review and an expression of hope for the improvement of the relations with foreign states. A close scrutiny of all such speeches delivered at the twenty-five prorogations preceding royal proclamations for dissolution [26] reveals that, with the possible exception of the speech given at the prorogation of August 16, 1832, the general practice in the nineteenth century was definitely to announce the impending dissolution of Parliament in a Speech from the Throne. [27] With the dawn of the present century, however,

[26] In the prorogation preceding the dissolution of Parliament in 1895, the Speech from the Throne was not officially recorded either in the *Journals of the House of Lords* or in *Hansard,* so that it is unknown whether the impending dissolution was referred to in the Speech or not.

[27] When Parliament was prorogued on August 15, 1834, and again on August 5, 1873, dissolution was then not contemplated; so that the Speech from the Throne on both occasions only announced the termination of the session and the royal desire to release the Lords and Commons from attendance. On the former occasion, it said: "I at length close this protracted Session, and release you from your attendance" [25 *Hansard* (Lords) 3 s., 1265-1269]; while on the latter, it said: "I am now released from the necessity of calling upon you for the further prosecution of your arduous occupations" [217 *Hansard* (Lords) 3 s., 1555-9]. The prorogation held on August 16, 1832, took place under entirely different circumstances, because with the passing of the Reform Bill it had been a foregone conclusion that Parliament should be dissolved in order to put the new law into operation. Yet, on that occasion, the Speech from the Throne did not expressly mention that Parliament would be dissolved. As in 1834 and 1873 or any other occasion when

this practice, which had prevailed during almost the entire Victorian period, has been gradually discarded.   Since 1900 it has been customary to make no reference to the impending dissolution of Parliament.   The nearest approach to an announcement was an appeal to the people in the Speech made in 1918 and in 1931, for co-operation in each case, with an emergency government for carrying the nation through a national crisis; [28] whereas the Speech of November, 1910 and that of 1923, while not mentioning the dissolution itself, alluded in each case to its cause.[29]

After the delivery of the Speech from the Throne, the Commission for proroguing the Parliament [30] was read, in

Parliament was prorogued by the Crown without an intention to dissolve, it just stated: "The state of the public business now enabling me to release you from a further attendance in Parliament. . ." 114 *Hansard* (Lords) 3 s., 1312-1416.

[28] On November 21, 1918, it was stated in "His Majesty's Speech" that "through the extension of the suffrage which this Parliament has carried into effect, all classes of My People will have an opportunity of inspiring and guiding this beneficient undertaking (repairing of the ravages of war and restoring of national prosperity)." 32 *H. L. Deb.* 5 s., 371-74.

On October 7, 1931, it was said in the same kind of speech that "I am confident that, as on former occasions in the history of the country, every citizen will co-operate to the utmost of his power in restoring prosperity to the nation." 82 *H. L. Deb.* 5 s., 300-302.

[29] The speech of November 28, 1910 said: "I regret that the Conference which took place with a view to arriving at a solution of the recurring difficulties between the two Houses of Parliament has failed to come to an agreement." (6 *H. L. Deb.* 5 s., 1013-1016.) Like that speech, the speech of November 16, 1923, also referred to the cause of dissolution by saying: "The position of agriculture and the problem of unemployment throughout the country continue to cause Me deep anxiety. Despite all the efforts of My Government to stimulate trade and to alleviate distress, the circumstances of large numbers of our fellow-citizens still remain deplorable. My Ministers are convinced that unless measures for safe-guarding and development of the home market are adopted, no permanent improvement in their situation can be expected." 55 *H. L. Deb.* 5 s., 39-42.

[30] For an example, see *Journals of H. L.* (1930-31), vol. 163, pp. 380-1.

case Parliament was prorogued by Commission instead of by the sovereign in person. By virtue of such Commission the Lord Chancellor then proceeded to announce the prorogation of Parliament until a certain day. When this was over, the sovereign, in case of prerogation in person, would descend the Throne and leave the House. In case of prorogation by Commission the Lords Commissioners, as described by MacDonagh, would " shake hands with the Lord Chancellor and withdraw to their robing-rooms behind the Throne. The Lord Chancellor, gathering up his long robes, and attended by the Purse-bearer and the Mace-bearer, walks down the floor to the Bar, and also disappears." The Speaker and Commons, who had been summoned to the House of Lords only about a quarter of an hour before, then also left. Having returned to the House of Commons without the mace " the Speaker walks up the floor of the Chamber bowing to the empty Chair. Then, standing at the head of the Table, he tells the Commons (standing around) that he has been to the House of Lords, and reads the King's speech, with the contents of which they are already acquainted. Not a word is officially said, as a rule, about the forthcoming dissolution. . . . And so the Speaker, lingering awhile by the Chair, shakes hands with the Members that surround him and wishes them good fortune in the approaching battle in the constituencies. Then he disappears from the Chamber." With the subsequent retirement of the Serjeant-at-Arms with the Mace, all that could be heard in the House was the rustling of papers which the Clerks were collecting from the Table and the voice of the doorkeeper in the lobby shouting " Who goes home? " echoed by the policemen in all the corridors of the Palace of Westminster.[31] Subsequently, the royal proclamation " For Dis-

[31] MacDonagh, *The Pageant of Parliament* (London, 1921) vol. ii, pp. 237-238.

solving the Present Parliament, and Declaring the Calling
of Another " would be issued by the sovereign " by and with
the advice of Our Privy Council," [32] while Parliament stood
prorogued. This proclamation discharges the existing Parliament from its duties of attendance, declares the desire of
the Crown to have the advice of its people and the royal will
and pleasure to call a new Parliament and further announces
an Order addressed by the Crown in Council to the Chancellors of Great Britain and Ireland—since 1922, to " Our
Chancellor of Great Britain and Our Governor of Northern
Ireland " [33]—to issue the necessary writs, this proclamation
to be their authority for so doing.[34]

With the prorogation of Parliament and the proclamation
of dissolution, the House of Lords as well as the House of
Commons is brought to an end.[35]   But, the position of the

[32] For an example, see *Journals of H. L.* (1930-31), vol. 163, p. 381.

[33] The Irish settlement of 1922 made no provision for the election of
Irish representative peers; and since the office of Lord Chancellor of
Ireland has been abolished, there is no one to whom, under provision
of the Act of Union, 1800, a writ for the election of a representative
peer can legally be addressed. (Ogg, *English Government and Politics,*
p. 321, fn. 18.) As a result, no Irish representative peers have been
chosen since the creation of the Irish Free State; and at the beginning
of 1933, the number of such peers in the House of Lords had dwindled
from the original twenty-eight to eighteen. *Constitutional Year Book,*
1933, p. 123.

[34] " Until recent times it was the practice for a warrant under the
sign manual to be given by the Crown to the Chancellor to issue the
necessary writs. This has ceased to be done: an order in Council is
made directing that writs should be issued, but, as a matter of fact, the
Royal Proclamation is treated by the Crown Office in Chancery as the
authority for the issue." Anson, *Law and Custom of the Constitution,*
vol. i, p. 53.

[35] During the dissolution, it is, however, lawful, under the provision
of the Appellate Jurisdiction Act, 1876, for the sovereign, by writing
under his sign manual, " to authorize the Lords of Appeal in the House
of Lords to hear and determine appeals . . . , and for that purpose to

Lords as members of Parliament is not thereby affected.
Although only by virtues of fresh writs issued to them from
the Crown office can they return to their seats in the House
of Lords,[36] yet according to various judicial decisions and
resolutions of the Lords based thereon in the seventeenth century these writs cannot be denied by the Crown.[37] Exceptions to this rule may, however, be found in the power, as
given by the Titles Deprivation Act, 1917, " to remove from
the peerage roll any peer reported by a Committee of the

sit in the House of Lords at such times as may be thought expedient."
39 & 40 Vict., c. 59.

In this connection, it may be worth while to note the fact, dealt with
by Sir William Anson in his *Law and Custom of The Constitution*, that
the judges, and the Attorney- and Solicitor-General, are summoned for
the ordinary Parliamentary sessions as well as during the dissolution,
"but in an inferior capacity. Their writs are writs ' of *Attendance* '
not ' of *Summons* '. They are not invited to be present ' *with* the said
Prelates, Peers, and the Great Men ' but with Us and with the rest of
our Council to treat and give your advice'. It is in virtue of this writ
of attendance that the Judges are called upon to give their opinions on
difficult points of law which come before the House of Lords as a
Court of Appeal. But they do not come as Peers of Parliament, and
recent procedure in the matter of their summons shows that it is
regarded rather as an obligation than as a dignity." Vol. i, pp. 58-9.

[36] The writs issued by the Crown Office are addressed to five different
classes of persons: 1. Writ of Summons to a Temporal Peer of England,
2. Writ of Summons to a Spiritual Peer, 3. Writ of Attendance addressed
to the Judges, and the Attorney- and Solicitor-General, 4. Writ addressed
to the Sheriff or Returning Officer of a County or borough for the
election of a member of the House of Commons, and 5. Writ addressed
to the twenty-eight temporal peers of Ireland (*cf. supra*, p. 122, fn. 33).
As for the Scotch representative peers, they do not receive a writ of
summons; their election is made in pursuance of a separate Proclamation issued under the Great Seal of Great Britain in accordance with a
statute passed in 1707 (6 Anne, c. 23). The sixteen elected Scotch
peers, after their election, present themselves to take the oath, which is
preliminary to taking their seats in right of their election as evidenced
by the list supplied to the Clerk of the House of Lords by the Lord
Clerk Register of Scotland through the clerk of the Crown in Chancery.
Cf. Anson, *op. cit.*, vol. i, pp 54-58, 219-221.

[37] Anson, *Ibid.*, vol. i, pp. 201-202.

Privy Council appointed for the purpose to have adhered to the King's enemies during the late war; " [38] and also in the limitation, as provided by the Bankruptcy Disqualification Act, 1871, that "a writ of summons shall not be issued to any peer for the time disqualified from sitting or voting in the House of Lords." [39]

With the House of Commons, however, it is entirely different. Few of its members have any certainty of coming back from the country. "Who goes home?", a symbol of Parliamentary pageantry, resounds through the vaulted halls just as it did at the end of an ordinary night sitting of the House of Commons; but on this occasion it is a question tragically addressed to many, for their prevailing fear at the close of a Parliament is whether they are going home to stay or will soon return to their seats in the House of Commons.

[38] Anson, *Law and Custom of the Constitution* (5th ed., Oxford, 1922), vol. i, p. 226.

MacDonagh said: "During the World War the Crown exercised the discretion of not issuing writs of summons to the Duke of Cumberland and the Duke of Albany, as they had joined the King's enemies . . . the Germans." *The Pageant of Parliament*, vol. ii, p. 237.

[39] Anson, *op. cit.*, vol. i, p. 226.

The Crown's right of summons is further limited "by the rule that only a British subject (whether born of English parents or naturalized) may receive a writ of summons to the House of Lords". *Ibid.*

CHAPTER V

RESIGNATION OF THE MINISTRY AND DISSOLUTION
OF PARLIAMENT

IN case of the demise of the Crown Parliament was, before
1867, as we have said, automatically brought to an end, but
the existence of the ministry was left to the discretion of the
new sovereign. According to an act of Parliament, passed
in 1707 and still in force, the Privy Council, which includes,
of course, the Cabinet ministers, "shall not be determined
or dissolved by the death or demise of her Majesty (Queen
Anne was then on the throne), her heirs or successors; but
such privy council shall continue and act as such by the space
of six months next after such demise . . . unless sooner
determined by the next successor" to the throne. Specific
mention was made of certain important offices, among them
being those of the Lord Chancellor, the "Lord High Treas-
urer," the Lord President of the Council, the Lord Privy
Seal and the "Lord High Admiral." [1] However, the Ministers of the Crown were, as a rule, reappointed by the new
sovereign upon his accession to the throne. [2] Moreover,
since the Cabinet as such is, as we have said, [3] wholly unknown to the law, there is no legal provision to prescribe
its duration, as in the case of Parliament. The rule has
however been established through conventions [4] that the
Cabinet shall remain in power so long as it enjoys the confidence of the House of Commons and that it may at any
time be forced out of office through the withdrawal of such

---

[1] 6 Anne, c. 7.

[2] MacDonagh, *The Pageant of Parliament*, vol. ii, pp. 224-225.

[3] See *supra*, p. 25.

[4] Dicey, *Introduction to the Study of the Law of the Constitution*
(London, 1889), p. 300.

confidence. Upon the manifestation by a ruling majority in the House of Commons of its displeasure with the Cabinet, the natural alternative to resignation is an appeal to the country by the Cabinet, which is vested with the right to advise and request the sovereign to dissolve Parliament.[5] Analysis of the process of the dissolution of Parliament would therefore not be complete without a brief review of the resignation of ministries and a more detailed discussion of their relation to the dissolution of Parliament.

During the hundred years under discussion there have been thirty-seven different ministries. Of these five were ended for non-political reasons, *viz.,* one through the death of the first minister (Lord Palmerston in 1865)[6] and four[7] through the resignation of the first minister because of ill-health (Lord Derby in 1868,[8] Lord Salisbury in 1902,[9] Sir Henry Campbell-Bannerman in 1908,[10] and Mr. Bonar Law in 1923.)[11] The remaining thirty-two fell for political reasons of one kind or another.

[5] This is not, of course, the *only* alternative. In case of a defeat on a major bill in the House of Commons the ministry has more often preferred to bear up under rebuffs than to make it a ground for resignation or dissolution. [*Cf.* 150 *Hansard* (Commons) 4 s., 49 *et seq.*]. It may also "deny the finality of the judgment and reverse the hostile vote" at a later stage, or it may "take shelter under a general vote of confidence" to be introduced by one of the Ministerialists. Morley, *Life of Gladstone,* vol. ii, pp. 207-208.

[6] 184 *Hansard* (Lords) 3 s., 653-660.

[7] In tendering his resignation to Queen Victoria on March 3, 1894, Gladstone mentioned "the condition of his sight and hearing, both of them impaired" as the reason for relinquishing his office (*Letters of Queen Victoria, 1886-1901,* vol. ii, pp. 371-372) ; but actually the breakup of his Cabinet was due chiefly to difference of opinion between him and the majority of his colleagues on matters of navy estimates and dissolution. See *supra,* pp. 38-39.

[8] Monypenny and Buckle, *Life of Disraeli,* vol. iv, pp. 582-590.

[9] Lee, *King Edward VII,* vol. ii, pp. 158-159.

[10] Spender, *Life of Henry Campbell-Bannerman,* vol. ii, pp. 387-389.

[11] Fitzroy, *Memoirs,* vol. ii, p. 806.

As we found when examining the problem of dissolution so we find on turning to that of resignation only one case where the sovereign's direct intervention is a sufficient explanation of what happened. This was of course the dismissal of Melbourne in 1834, on the ground that the ministers were "not strong enough in the Commons to carry on the business of the country,"[12] an event that led directly to the dissolution of the same year which we have discussed in Chapter III.

During the reign of Queen Victoria, however, resignations of the ministry were caused chiefly by defeats in the House of Commons. In the hundred years since the Reform of 1832 only ten of the ministries that could normally command a majority in the House of Commons resigned because of such defeats[13] and these resignations all occurred while

[12] See *supra*, pp. 43-45.

[13]

Date of Defeat	Head of Government Defeated	Source of Material about the Defeat and the Subsequent Resignation
May 6, 1839	Lord Melbourne	47 *Hansard* (Commons) 3 s., 871-972, 975-978
June 25, 1846	Sir Robert Peel	87 *Hansard* (Commons) 3 s., 966-1032, 1040-1055
Feb. 20, 1851	Lord John Russell	114 *Hansard* (Commons) 3 s., 850-871, 892-895
Feb. 20, 1852	Lord John Russell	119 *Hansard* (Commons) 3 s., 838-876, 887-888
Jan. 29, 1855	Lord Aberdeen	136 *Hansard* (Commons) 3 s., 1121-1233, 1260-1262
Feb. 19, 1858	Lord Palmerston	148 *Hansard* (Commons) 3 s., 1741-1847, 1868
June 18, 1866	Lord John Russell	184 *Hansard* (Commons) 3 s., 536-643, 684-692
March 11, 1873	Mr. Gladstone	214 *Hansard* (Commons) 3 s., 1741-1868, 1909
June 8, 1885	Mr. Gladstone	298 *Hansard* (Commons) 3 s., 1417-1515, 1528-1531
June 21, 1895	Lord Rosebery	34 *Hansard* (Commons) 4 s., 1673-1712, 1746-1748

Queen Victoria was on the throne. In this connection the point that especially interests us is the question whether it is possible to explain, in common terms, the reasons why the defeated ministries should have resorted to resignation instead of dissolution when adoption of the latter course was within their discretion. In order to answer this question, it is necessary to describe briefly the various particular situations involved and therefrom ascertain the causes that led these ministries to relinquish their offices instead of dissolving the disaffected House of Commons.

First of all, in the much-discussed case of 1839 in which the Melbourne Government resigned, taking a majority of five for the government on the Jamaica Government Bill as an indication of want of confidence [14] we notice that at the time of the ministry's resignation "troubles from all quarters," in Disraeli's words, had pressed "simultaneously upon them: Canadian revolts, Chartist insurrections, Chinese squabbles and mysterious complications in Central Asia which threatened immediate hostilities with Persia, and even with one of the most powerful of European Empires. In addition to all this, the revenue continuously declined, and every day the general prejudice became more intense against the Irish policy of the Ministry." [15]   On March 21 the government was defeated in the House of Lords by a vote of 63 to 58 on a motion proposed by the Earl of Roden for an inquiry into the state of Ireland, and on April 15, the government's majority in the House of Commons on Lord John Russell's resolution concerning Ireland was reduced to twenty-two. The latter vote was regarded by Sir Robert Peel, the leader of the Opposition, as "morally a defeat. England and Scotland had pronounced against them (min-

[14] 47 *Hansard* (Lords) 3 s., 973-974.

[15] Monypenny and Buckle, *Life of Disraeli*, vol. ii, p. 54.

isters.) " [16] Under such circumstances it would not have
been of much use to the government, which was gradually
deprived of the support of a section of the extreme Liberals
and which had been able to tide over the session of 1838
only under the shadow of the extremely popular sovereign,[17]
to make a plea to the people for support after a further
dwindling of its majority in the House of Commons on the
Jamaica Government Bill.

The resignation of the Peel Government in 1846 was a
result of defeat in the House of Commons on the Protection
of Life (Ireland) Bill, through the combined opposition of
the Protectionists led by Disraeli and Lord George Bentinck
and of a section of Whigs led by Lord John Russell.[18] This
occurred on June 25, 1846, the very day on which the Corn
Law Repeal Bill received a third reading in the House of
Lords without a division. It has been revealed in " Sir
Robert Peel's Memorandum on the position of the Government, June 21 " of the same year [19] that he at that time
deprecated nothing more than the dissolution of Parliament
on the express ground of the Irish Coercion Bill, because it
might, he thought, constitute, among other things, an appeal
to the constituencies of Great Britain against those of Ireland.
Moreover, he realized the impossibility of openly uniting
with the Liberals against the Protectionists with " free trade
and the Destruction of Protection " as a slogan. The " in-
superable difficulty," as he called it, was the sugar question.
If the avowed intention of the government to propose the
continuance for a month of the existing sugar duties, which

[16] Duke of Buckingham and Chandos, *Memoirs of the Courts and
Cabinets of William IV and Victoria* (London, 1861), vol. ii, pp. 378-381.

[17] Monypenny and Buckle, *op. cit.*, vol. ii, p. 54.

[18] *Gathorne Hardy, First Earl of Cranbrook, A Memoir* (London,
1910), vol. i, p. 56; Maxwell, *Life of Wellington,* vol. ii, pp. 352-353.

[19] *Memoirs by Sir Robert Peel,* vol. ii, pp. 288-297.

would otherwise expire on the fifth of the following July, was to be adhered to, Parliament could not be dissolved without another temporary Sugar Bill, for Parliament after a General Election could not assemble before the fifth of August. The necessity of asking for the continuance for three months of the sugar duties would compel the Ministerialists to hoist the banner of " Free Trade, but not in sugar," while that of the Liberals would " bear upon it the plain, intelligible motto of 'Free Trade without Restriction '." In that case, there would be no hope that the government opposed on the one hand by Protectionists and on the other by the advocates of Free Trade—of Free Trade without qualification or reserve—would be able to obtain a majority. Incidentally, he expressed the following opinion regarding what he called " Justification of dissolution ":

I think no Ministers ought to advise the Sovereign to dissolve Parliament without feeling a moral conviction that Dissolution will enable them to carry on the Government of the country— will give them a Parliament with a decided working majority of supporters. The hope of getting a stronger minority is no justification of Dissolution.

Unsuccessful Dissolutions are, generally speaking, injurious to the authority of the Crown. Following rapidly one after the other, they blunt the edge of a great instrument given to the Crown for its protection.

In announcing the resignation of his government in the House of Commons on June 24, 1846, Sir Robert Peel [20] said that in the existing state and divisions of party and after all that had occurred, he did not entertain a confident hope that a dissolution would give him a decided working majority of supporters in the new House of Commons. His government had, therefore, preferred instant resignation to the alternative of dissolution.

[20] 87 *Hansard* (Commons) 3 s., 1040-1055.

The Russell Government which succeeded the Peel Government in 1846 was defeated five years later on Locke King's motion on County Franchise through the action of its unruly followers, the Radicals, while the Conservatives had " moved off almost in a body." [21] This led to the resignation of the Russell Government. The causes which produced the feeling of the House against Lord Russell and indirectly led to his resignation were, according to Baron Stockmar, " only to be found in the Papal Aggression " in September, 1850,[22] which resulted in the introduction on February 7, 1851 by Lord Russell of the Ecclesiastical Tithes Bill, a Bill giving offence to " all parties " including Protestants, Irish Catholics and Liberal followers of the government. Consequently, when he " went over the ground of a possible demand for a dissolution " with Queen Victoria and Prince Albert after his defeat on Locke King's motion, they all agreed that such a demand might, as recorded by Prince Albert on February 22, 1851, "bring on a general commotion in the country." Therefore, since he considered that he " could not go on " with the government, the only alternative left was to relinquish his office.[23]

The much weakened Russell government, recalled to office in March 1851, after Lord Russell himself, in conjunction with Lord Aberdeen and Sir James Graham, the Peelites, and later Lord Stanley had each in turn failed to form a new government,[24] found itself in a still more difficult position during the latter part of the year when Lord Palmerston, whose " prestige in the House " was then, in Disraeli's words, " very great; in the country, considerable," [25] was dismissed

[21] Monypenny and Buckle, *Life of Disraeli*, vol. iii, pp. 285-6.

[22] *Memoirs of Baron Stockmar*, vol. ii, pp. 445-450.

[23] *Letters of Queen Victoria, 1837–1861*, vol. ii, pp. 346-352.

[24] Maxwell, *Life and Letters of the Fourth Earl of Clarendon*, vol. i, p. 324.

[25] Monypenny and Buckle, *Life of Disraeli*, vol. iii, p. 342.

as Foreign Minister. "Once again the Peelites were invited to enter the Ministry and once again they declined." [26] The situation had then become such that, as Lord Russell himself said, it was no longer possible to carry on the administration: [27]

I felt it to be my duty to declare the political connection between Lord Palmerston and myself to be dissolved. But I felt at the same time that my Government was so much weakened that it was not likely to retain power for any long time. Accordingly, I took the first opportunity to resign office.

"The first opportunity" was the defeat of the government on Lord Palmerston's amendment to the Militia Bill. Fully aware of the division among the Whigs and greatly humiliated by "the almost insulting manner toward him in which the House by its cheers," as Lord Palmerston expressed it, "went with me in the debate," [28] Lord Russell tendered the resignation of his government by informing the Queen that [29] "the Cabinet had been unanimous that there was no other course to pursue, and that it would not be advisable to make use of the Queen's permission to advise a Dissolution."

The Aberdeen Government, formed at the end of 1852 with the support of the Whigs and the Free Trade followers of Sir Robert Peel to displace the short-lived Conservative government under Lord Derby which had succeeded the Russell Government in February, 1852, resigned in February, 1855 on a defeat on Mr. Roebuck's motion that "a select Committee be appointed to inquire into the condition of our Army before Sebastopol, and into the conduct of those De-

[26] *The Later Correspondence of Lord John Russell, 1840–1878* (London, 1925), vol. i, p. xxxvi.

[27] Russell, *Recollections and Suggestions, 1813–1873*, p. 258.

[28] Ashley, *Life of Viscount Palmerston*, vol. i, pp. 334–335.

[29] *Letters of Queen Victoria, 1837–1861*, vol. ii, pp. 445–446.

partments of the Government whose duty it has been to minister to the wants of that Army." During the winter of the preceding year, when the allied forces of England and France were engaged with the Russians on the battlefield of the Crimea, transports laden with stores for the English troops were wrecked and their cargoes lost. The bitterness of the weather proved more terrible than the Russian sword, and the English force wasted away with cold and disease. The public indignation at the sufferings of its troops paved the ground for Mr. Roebuck, a Radical, to make the above mentioned motion condemning the Duke of Newcastle's administration of the war. On the mere notice of the motion Lord Russell, then Foreign Secretary, resigned on the ground that he could not resist it. Because of the desertion of the chief lieutenant in the Coalition Cabinet and the atmosphere of general condemnation in the country, Lord Aberdeen could not possibly resort to dissolution or any other course but resignation, after Russellite Whigs and Radicals as well as Conservatives had gone into the Opposition lobby on Mr. Roebuck's motion, thus producing a crushing majority of 157 (148 vs. 305) against his ministry.[80]

The Palmerston Government which succeeded was itself deprived of power three years later. The vote that drove Lord Palmerston to resignation was a majority of nineteen against him on the second reading of the Conspiracy Bill on February 19, 1858. It may appear strange that, only twenty-four hours before, his government should have been able to secure the handsome majority of 145 on the first reading of the Government of India Bill. As Lord Palmerston walked home after that division " he was told by Bethell, his Attorney-General, that, like a Roman Consul at a triumph, he ought to be accompanied by a slave to remind him of his

[80] *Cf.* Monypenny and Buckle, *Life of Disraeli*, vol. iii, pp. 555-557; Morley, *Life of Gladstone*, vol. i, pp. 521-525.

mortality." [31]   Long before the India Bill was voted upon, however, the "diminution of his popularity," as has been recorded in the *Greville Memoirs,* " was visible universally. This was attributed to several small causes, but the great one was the appointment of Clanricards [as Privy Seal after some unpleasant disclosures in the Irish Courts] which beyond all doubt has been regarded with a disgust and indignation to the last degree exaggerated and uncalled for." [32] But general dissatisfaction toward Lord Palmerston on this affair did not prove great enough to cost him his office. When, in response to the threats of Colonels of the French Army uttered following an unsuccessful attempt to assassinate the French Emperor and Empress, [33] he gave notice of his intention to bring in a Bill to amend the law of conspiracy, making conspiring to murder a felony punishable by penal servitude for life instead of a misdemeanour as provided by the existing law, the hardened hostility in Parliament and disapproval in the country suddenly appeared to be too strong

[31] Monypenny and Buckle, *op. cit.,* vol. iv, p. 110.

[32] *The Greville Memoirs, 1852–1860* (London, 1887), vol. ii, p. 163. Cf. *Letters of Queen Victoria, 1837–1861,* vol. iii, p. 338, fn. 1.

[33] On January 14, 1858, "an unsuccessful attempt, resulting, however, in the death of several onlookers, was made in Paris to assassinate with bombs the Emperor and Empress of the French. The Conspirators were Italians, members of the secret society of the Carbonari, to which Louis Napoleon had once himself belonged; but Orsini's plot had been concocted, and his bombs had been manufactured, in England. Very naturally, there was an outburst of anger in France against *perfide Albion,* who sheltered regicides. Colonels of the French army uttered violent threats, and their addresses were printed in the official *Moniteur.*" Monypenny and Buckle, *Life of Disraeli,* vol. iv, pp. 111-114. " The French Government addressed a . . . request to Queen Victoria's government that measures should be taken 'to provide such a guarantee of security which no state can refuse to a neighboring State, and which we are entitled to expect from an ally'." Accordingly, Lord Palmerston introduced the Conspiracy Bill referred to above. Maxwell, *Life and Letters of the Fourth Earl of Clarendon,* vol. ii, pp. 160-1.

to overcome. The threats of the French Colonels were followed by a despatch from Walewski, the Emperor's Foreign Minister, in which he pointedly asked, in reference to the said attempt, whether the right of asylum ought to protect " assassination reduced to a doctrine, preached openly, practiced in repeated attempts, the most recent of which has struck Europe with stupefaction." Although verbal communication did take place, the government neglected to make formal reply to this despatch, and the omission was strongly resented. The Conspiracy bill, on the first reading, was carried by a majority of two hundred, as the bulk of the Conservatives voted with the Ministers. Lord Derby, seeing that there were ninety-nine members, chiefly of the Liberal Party, who had voted against the government, then instructed his followers to vote against the Bill on Mr. Gibson's amendment which expressed no opinion on the Bill, but censured ministers for not answering Walewski's despatch before bringing in their Bill. As a result, the government was defeated by a combination consisting of " the whole of the Conservative Party . . . Lord John Russell, the Peelites, with Mr. Gladstone and the whole of the Radicals." [34] Under these circumstances and because of the fact that since the country had been appealed to only eleven months before (i. e. March 1857) " another dissolution was obviously out of the question," [35] Lord Palmerston had no alternative but to resign.

The next case of the resignation as a result of a defeat in the House of Commons of a ministry that could normally command a majority was that of the Russell Government

[34] *Letters of Queen Victoria, 1837-1861*, vol. iii, pp. 335-340; Monypenny and Buckle, *op. cit.*, vol. iv, pp. 111-114.

[35] Dasent, *John Thadeus Delane, His Life and Correspondence* (New York, 1908), vol. i, p. 281; and *cf.* Monypenny and Buckle, *op. cit.*, vol. iv, pp. 111-4.

on the defeat in Committee of the Representation of the People Bill by a majority of eleven (304 vs. 315) on June 18, 1866. "In this majority of eleven against the the government were found no fewer than forty-four of their professed supporters." [36] The Cabinet, after the defeat, was evenly divided on the alternatives that could be taken. [37] Dissolution was " only approved by three or four " ministers among whom was the Duke of Argyll, Lord Privy Seal, who shared the view of Mr. Bright who was not then a member of the government.　Among those who were strongly against having a new Parliament was Mr. Brand, the expert whip, who told Lord Russell that dissolution " would be unpopular with their own friends, who had been put to great expense at their election only a few months before.　It would, moreover, break the party, because at an election they would have to bring out men of more extreme views to fight the whigs and liberals who had deserted them on reform and who might thus be driven permanently to the other side." [38]　Lord Clarendon, then Foreign Secretary, also informed the Prime Minister on June 23, 1866, two days before resignation was decided upon, that he could not be a party to a dissolution which he believed " would do no good to the cause of Reform and would be fatal to the Liberal interest." [39]　Mr. Glad-

[36] Morley, *Life of Gladstone*, vol. ii, p. 206.

[37] It was recorded by Mr. Gladstone on June 25, 1866 as follows: " Cabinet 2½-4½. . . . The final position appeared to be this, as to alternatives before the Cabinet. 1. Dissolution, only approved by three or four. 2. A vote of confidence with vague assurance as to future reform . . . desired by seven, one more acquiescing reluctantly, six opposing. W. E. G. *unable to act on it.* 3. Lord Russell's proposal to rehabilitate the clause . . . disapproved by seven, approved by six, two ready to acquiesce. 4. Resignation generally accepted, hardly any strongly dissenting . . . " *Ibid.*, vol. ii, p. 209.

[38] *Ibid.*, vol. ii, pp. 207-209.

[39] Maxwell, *Life and Letters of the Fourth Earl of Clarendon*, vol. ii, pp. 315-316.

stone, the Chancellor of the Exchequer, was, as reported by John Morley, "on the morrow of the defeat, for resignation," a course of action which in later years he regretted having taken.[40]   As for the Prime Minister himself, he proposed to revive the clause of the Bill on which the government had been defeated with the expectation that the hostile vote would be reversed on report; but his proposal was "disapproved by seven" of his colleagues.   On June 26, the day after resignation had been finally accepted by the Cabinet, the Prime Minister announced in the House of Lords that after the defeat on the Representation of the People Bill his government did not intend to carry on because they did not want to forfeit "pledges we had given to the country and to Parliament to bring in a Reform Bill which we might expect to carry." [41]   Moreover, because of the general apathy on the subject of reform, especially in the South of England, the Cabinet, as Lord Russell had already reported to the Queen on June 19 and June 22, was also averse to a dissolution; [42] so that the only course left for the ministers was to tender their resignations of the offices they held.

After an interim of two and a half years from Lord Russell's resignation in June, 1866, the Liberals again came into power.   The government formed by Mr. Gladstone in 1868 resigned as a result of defeat in the House of Commons, following slightly more than four years in office.   An an-

---

[40] Morley, *op. cit.*, vol. ii, pp. 207-209.

However, according to Mr. Gladstone's letter of June 20, 1866 to Lord Russell, recently revealed, Gladstone told the Prime Minister only two days after the government's defeat that "the reasons against dissolution seem to lie on the surface" and, in his view, dissolution was "the course most conformable to the principles and spirit of the Constitution." *Later Correspondence of Lord John Russell, 1840-1878*, vol. ii, p. 315.

[41] 184 *Hansard* (Lords) 3 s., 653-660.

[42] *Letters of Queen Victoria, 1862-1878*, vol. i, pp. 335-342.

alysis of the vote (284 for and 287 against the Gladstone
Government) on the second reading of the Irish University
Bill on March 11, 1873 reveals that the government " had a
small majority among the English members, and a large
majority among the Scotch; but the Irish voted 68 to 15
against them." [43]   From the point of view of parties, it was
" due to Liberal defections rather than to Conservative
machinations." [44]   An explanation of the preference for resignation to dissolution is found in Mr. Gladstone's own words
as follows: [45]

Friday March 13. I . . . went to the Cabinet at 12:15.
Stated the case between the two alternatives of resignation and
dissolution as far as regarded myself.   On the side of resignation it would not be necessary to make any final announcement [of his retirement from the leadership.]   I am strongly
advised a temporary rest.   On the other hand, if we now dissolve, I anticipate that *afterwards* before any long time difficulties will arise, and my mission will be terminated.   So that the
alternatives are not so unequally weighed.   The Cabinet without
any marked difference, or at least without any positive assertion
to the contrary, determined on tendering their resignations.

Later, when Mr. Disraeli, the leader of the Opposition, refused to take office the Gladstone Ministry was compelled
once more to take the reins of government. [46]

In regard to the resignations of the Gladstone Government
in 1885 and the Rosebery Government in 1895, a word or
two may suffice for our purpose here, since they have been
analyzed in some detail elsewhere. [47]   In the former case,
resignation was preferred to dissolution not only because of

[43] Monypenny and Buckle, *Life of Disraeli*, vol. v, p. 206.

[44] Ponsonby, *Side Lights on Queen Victoria*, p. 126.

[45] Morley, *Life of Gladstone*, vol. ii, pp. 446-447.

[46] See *supra*, p. 95.

[47] See *supra*, pp. 78-80.

the decline of the government's popularity in the country owing to the unsuccessful campaign in Egypt and the Soudan, the loss at by-elections, the hostility of the Irish Home Rulers to renewal of the Crimes Act of 1882 and their alliance with the Tories in defeating the government on the Budget, but also because of the fact that "an immediate dissolution" after the government's defeat, as Alfred E. Gathorne Hardy saw it, "was really impossible, as the new electorate created by the Reform Bill had not yet come into existence and the old one was practically superseded." [48] As for the other case, it may be said that Lord Rosebery chose resignation rather than dissolution for a number of reasons. His government had sustained constant loss at by-elections and had been deprived of the support of the Parnellite Irish Nationalists. Furthermore, the ministry had been defeated on an amendment to the Army estimate providing a reduction of the salary of the Secretary for War by one hundred pounds. [49] A dissolution could not take place until the Army Vote was passed but the Army Vote could not be passed without a successor to Mr. Campbell-Bannerman as Secretary for War. The Cabinet might conceivably have thrown over Mr. Campbell-Bannerman and substituted another minister, but failing that their only course was to resign. [50] Moreover, a tactical advantage was expected through putting the Conservatives in, thus making them bear the responsibility of government and disclose their policy before the dissolution. This plan was adopted also by Mr. Balfour in 1905; but on neither occasion did it succeed. [51]

[48] Alfred E. Gathorne Hardy, *Gathorne Hardy, First Earl of Cranbook*, vol. ii, p. 214.

[49] 34 *Hansard* (Commons) 4 s., 1673-1712.

[50] Lucy, *A Diary of the Home Rule Parliament, 1892-1895* (London, 1896), pp. 479-480.

[51] Griffith-Boscawen, *Fourteen Years in Parliament*, pp. 69-74.

From the above analysis of the conditions involved in the ten resignations, after defeats in the House of Commons, of ministries which normally commanded a majority, we can see that a cabinet, after being defeated in the House of Commons, generally prefers resignation to dissolution if it feels that it has lost the support of the country or if it has suffered a defection of party-supporters. Sometimes, hostile public opinion in the country has been clearly manifested, as in the unfavourable returns of by-elections in 1880-1885 and in 1892-1895. Defection in the party in power might take the form of a break-up of the Cabinet through the retirement of some important member of the government, as in the dismissal of Lord Palmerston in 1852 and the resignation of Lord Russell in 1855. In only two instances where a defeated ministry relinquished its office instead of dissolving the House of Commons, i. e., in 1858 and in 1866, did the constitutional principle that repeated and frequent dissolutions are usually undesirable and therefore ought to be avoided come into consideration when a defeated ministry was at the cross-roads between resignation and dissolution.

In connection with the above analysis, we may also remark that, of the ten resignations already referred to, three did not materialize—Lord Melbourne was recalled to office after his resignation in 1839 because Sir Robert Peel, owing to the influence of the sovereign, could not be installed as Prime Minister to succeed him; [52] Lord Russell was recalled in 1851

[52] In May, 1839 the government of Lord Melbourne resigned on defeat in the House of Commons upon the Jamaica Bill. Queen Victoria upon the Duke of Wellington's advice sent for Sir Robert Peel. In his interview with the Queen, Sir Robert demanded that some of the Ladies of her Household, all of whom were connected with the Whig Party should be replaced by others representing the party of which he was the chief. The Queen, then not twenty years old, resented this and refused to adopt "a course which she conceives to be contrary to usage and which is repugnant to her feelings"—these words which were addressed by the Queen to Sir Robert were, by the way, not her own but were drafted by Lord Melbourne. For a while, the Queen parted with Sir Robert. The

when it had become evident that no new government could be formed either by Lord Russell himself in conjunction with the Peelites or by Lord Stanley; and Mr. Gladstone was recalled in 1873 when Disraeli had shown both his unwillingness to take office without a dissolution and his unwillingness to advise a dissolution if he should be installed in office. Of the remaining seven cases, the dismissals of the ministry in 1852, 1885, and 1895 by the House of Commons ultimately proved to be the death warrants of Parliament as well. Consequently, on only four occasions after the Reform of 1832, i. e., in 1846, 1855, 1858, and 1866 did Parliament successfully dismiss a ministry, that could normally command a majority, without precipitating its own dissolution. Since 1866, that is, for two-thirds of a century, no such dismissal has taken place.

A further interesting point becomes clear if we look at the above-mentioned seven cases from the standpoint of the political homogeneity of the majority upon which the government had rested. The Aberdeen Government which resigned in 1855 was a coalition supported by Whigs and Peelites. The Liberal Government that resigned in 1895 had at no time possessed an independent majority in the Parliament elected in 1892 [53] being maintained in office by the

Whig Government returned to office, and for two years longer remained the Counsellors of the sovereign. The matter was finally settled, before Sir Robert's accession to power in 1841, through the medium of Prince Albert by the retirement of the Duchessess of Bedford and Sutherland, and of Lady Normanby, which the Tories considered essential on account of their relationship to leading Whig Ministers—"an arrangement which, while it satisfied every fair requirement of the Tory Cabinet, involved no compromise of the principle for which Her Majesty had contended in 1839, that it was no part of the province of Ministers to say who should or should not be the Ladies of Her Household." Martin, *Life of the Prince Consort* (London, 1875), vol. i, pp. 105-106; and cf. *Letters of Queen Victoria, 1837-1861*, vol. i, pp. 178, 194-217, 341-345, and 358-359.

[53] The result of the General Election of 1892 was: Conservatives, 268;

support of the Nationalists. Thus since the Reform of 1832 Parliament has only five times dismissed a ministry that was normally able to command an *independent* and *homogeneous* majority, i. e., in 1846, 1852, 1858, 1866 and 1885. Nearly half a century has elapsed since the last such dismissal.

Having analyzed the various conditions under which ministries that have been defeated in the House of Commons chose resignation rather than dissolution, we now turn to a discussion of the reasons why certain ministries, when defeated, have preferred dissolution to resignation. Of the six dissolutions directly resulting from defeats in the House of Commons, referred to in Chapter III, that of 1841, owing to the very complex situation involved, perhaps merits the closest scrutiny. The situation preceding the government's defeat was, as recorded by Monypenny in the *Life of Disraeli*, such that " bad harvests and bad trade, aided by the business incapacity of the Government and by an adventurous foreign policy, had brought the finances of the country into serious disorder, deficit following deficit till the total reached millions. The Whigs in desperation sought an exit from their difficulties in a tentative advance towards the principles of free trade." [54] Hence, the Budget provided for a reduction of the duties on foreign sugar and timber, and the substitution of a fixed duty of a shilling a bushel on corn for the sliding scale previously in use. " These proposals . . . excited quite as much animosity among the protected interests as if the Government had proposed the abolition of all differential duties on sugar and timber, and a total repeal of the Corn Laws. The landed gentry and the farmers were especially indignant." [55] This unfavourable public opinion in the

Liberal Unionists, 47; Gladstonian Liberals, 274 and Nationalists, 81. *The Constitutional Year Book*, 1933, pp. 255-256.

[54] Monypenny and Buckle, *Life of Disraeli*, vol. ii, pp. 110-112.

[55] Russell, *Recollections and Suggestions, 1813-1873*, p. 206.

country, coupled with the losses sustained by the government at by-elections, impelled Lord Melbourne, before the Budget was voted upon, to resolve to resign his office in case of a defeat. He was then against dissolution because he thought that to try a dissolution " without succeeding in it," as he told Queen Victoria more than once, " would be to place your Majesty and ourselves in a worse situation than that in which we are at present." [56] Later on, however, when he learned that the Conservatives would dissolve, should they be installed in office, he informed the Queen that " if that was so *we must dissolve,* for then . . . it would come to just the same thing and . . . that changed my opinion very much." [57] But after the government had actually been defeated on the Budget, he changed his mind again and told the Queen: " I am still against dissolution. I don't think our chances of success are sufficient." [58] Finally his weak, vacillating mind was over-persuaded, and his objections to dissolution, apparently " personal to himself," as the Duke of Bedford remarked to Lord Russell, " on account of the very decided declarations he has made more than once in the House of Lords against agitating the Country on the corn question without a much stronger feeling in favour of change than he now possesses," [59] were overcome by the insistence of almost all of his colleagues in the Cabinet on the advisability of submitting the question of freedom of trade to the test of a General Election. [60]

With regard to the case of 1857, preference for dissolution to resignation was explained at considerable length by Lord Palmerston in the House of Commons and Lord Granville

[56] *Letters of Queen Victoria, 1836-1861,* vol. i, pp. 339 *et seq.*

[57] *Ibid.,* vol. i, pp. 350-351.

[58] *Ibid.,* vol. i, pp. 353-354.

[59] Walpole, *Life of Lord John Russell* (London, 1889), vol. i, p. 373.

[60] Russell, *op. cit.,* pp. 206-208.

in the House of Lords on March 5, 1857 when dissolution was announced.[61] Among the grounds mentioned was the fact that the state of parties, as shown by the vote on the Resolution on the China War and the votes on previous divisions, seemed to indicate that it would be extremely difficult for any government, whether the existing one or that which might be formed, to carry on the business of the country. As a matter of fact, however, the real reasons why a dissolution was preferred were not mentioned. A more plausible explanation of the preference was furnished by Lord Clarendon, then Foreign Secretary, through his letter of March 4, 1857 to Sir H. Seymour, the British Ambassador at Vienna. Lord Clarendon wrote: [62]

The best way would have been to dissolve or resign at once; but the latter was out of the question, *first,* because Palmerston is very popular and the country would have accused him of pusillanimity if he ran away from such an unholy alliance and had not given the people a chance of pronouncing . . .

Secondly. We could not resign against the wishes of the Queen, who, as her confinement approaches, is very nervous and in fact, *could* not undertake all the anxious duties that a change of government imposes upon the Sovereign. . . . We could not dissolve at once, because not a farthing has been voted nor has the Mutiny Act or any estimates been passed. We must therefore announce dissolution and get money voted for a short period. . . .

Of the points mentioned by Lord Clarendon, the fact that after the government's defeat the Queen signified her preference for a dissolution on account of her physical inability to go through with the anxiety of a change of government has already been discussed.[63] As for the personal popularity

[61] 144 *Hansard* (Commons) 3 s., 1894-1897; 144 *Hansard* (Lords) 3 s., 1885-1886.

[62] Maxwell, *Life and Letters of the Fourth Earl of Clarendon,* vol. ii, pp. 138-140.

[63] See *supra,* pp. 45-46.

of Lord Palmerston as a ground for dissolving Parliament, further proof may be found in the following message from Lord Palmerston to Queen Victoria on February 28, 1857: [64]

His (Lord Palmerston's) own firm belief is that the present Government has the confidence of the country in a greater degree that any other Government that could now be formed would have, and that consequently upon a Dissolution of Parliament, a House of Commons would be returned more favourable to the Government than the present.

Concerning the next case of dissolution as a result of defeat in the House of Commons, it may be said that, being a minority government, the Derby Ministry, (as Disraeli told Charles C. F. Greville, the Clerk of the Council, on April 20, 1859) " from the day of their taking office " in February, 1858, " had looked forward to a dissolution." [65] As early as May 16, 1858 when Lord Derby, being confronted with a vote of censure in both Houses of Parliament on a Despatch condemning the conduct of the Governor-General of India, asked Queen Victoria for her permission to announce that " in the event of an adverse majority, he had Her Majesty's sanction to a Dissolution of Parliament," [66] he justified his decision for a dissolution by saying that: [67]

. . . had he had to resign, he would have withdrawn from public business, and the Conservative Party would have been entirely, and he feared for ever, broken up. On a Dissolution he felt certain of a large gain, as the country was in fact tired of the " Whig Family Clique; " the Radicals, like Mr. Milner Gibson, Bright, etc., would willingly support a Conservative Government.

[64] *Letters of Queen Victoria, 1837-1861*, vol. iii, pp. 288-290.
[65] *The Greville Memoirs, 1852-1860*, vol. ii, p. 245.
[66] See *supra*, pp. 54-55.
[67] *Letters of Queen Victoria (1837-1861)*, vol. iii, pp. 367-368.

After the government's defeat on the Representation of the People Bill on March 31, 1859, dissolution became even more clearly the preferable alternative, because " a Parliament elected on a personal issue (i. e., for the support of Lord Palmerston), which signally defeated two (i. e., the Palmerston and the Derby) Ministries in two years, was a very unsatisfactory instrument of Government." [68] As it appeared to the Government just defeated, there was on the part of the members opposite no more ability to form or to maintain, should it be formed, an administration then than a year before when they retired from the Treasury Bench.   The lack of security for any government that might be formed and " almost a certainty that every February there will be a Ministerial crisis " would be " prejudicial to the repute of Parliament and injurious to the best interests of the country."   Believing, too, that the preservation of the peace of Europe during the struggle between Austria and the Franco-Sardinian allies [69] would " be seriously endangered by any change in the present composition of Her Majesty's Government " and " not being conscious " that the government has " done anything to forfeit the good opinion of our fellow countrymen," the ministers advised for a dissolution (with resignation as an alternative if it should not be approved) in order to let the country have an opportunity to pronounce its opinion on parliamentary reform and to supply a remedy for the existing unsatisfactory state of parties.[70]

Mr. Disraeli's preference for a dissolution in 1868 which was, as we have said,[71] partly due to insistence on the part

[68] Monypenny and Buckle, *Life of Disraeli*, vol. iv, p. 207.

[69] *Cf.* Morley, *Life of Gladstone*, vol. ii, pp. 5 *et seq.*

[70] 153 *Hansard* (Lords) 3 s., 1264-1291; 153 *Hansard* (Commons) 3 s., 1301-1307.

[71] See *supra*, pp. 46-47.

of Queen Victoria, was fully explained in his letter to the Queen on April 20, 1868, ten days before his government's defeat on Mr. Gladstone's first Resolution for the disestablishment of the Irish Church. Among the reasons mentioned therein and reasserted in another of his communications to the Queen on May 1, the next day after his government's defeat, was his intention to refer to the nation the new policy recommended by Mr. Gladstone. He said: [72]

It (the new policy) must produce great changes; according to the opinion of your Majesty's ministers, it may bring about serious consequences. They believe the opinion of the nation, after due consideration, will decide the new policy. . . .

In addition, it may be stated that the dissolution in 1868 was, in Mr. Asquith's words, the automatic consequence of extension of the franchise.[73] When Parliament was dissolved in the House of Lords on July 31, 1868, Lord Chancellor Cairns said on behalf of the Queen: [74]

It is my intention to dissolve the present Parliament at the earliest Day that will enable my People to reap the Benefits of the extended System of Representation which the Wisdom of Parliament has provided for them. . . .

It is perhaps needless to repeat that although the advice given to the Queen was to dissolve Parliament, an alternative tender was made of resignation which was not accepted by the Queen.[75]

With regard to Mr. Gladstone's decision for a dissolution after his government's defeat on the Home Rule Bill on June

[72] *Letters of Queen Victoria, 1862-1885*, vol. i, pp. 523-526; Monypenny and Buckle, *Life of Disraeli*, vol. v, pp. 29-32.

[73] Earl of Oxford and Asquith, *Fifty Years of British Parliament*, vol. ii, p. 218.

[74] 193 *Hansard* (Lords) 3 s., 1937-1940.

[75] Monypenny and Buckle, *op. cit.*, vol. v, pp. 32-33.

8, 1886, despite the fact that there had been a General Election only half a year before, reference may be made to the following passage in his biography by John Morley reciting what Gladstone said in the Cabinet the day following the defeat: [76]

He knew of no instance where a ministry defeated under circumstances like ours, upon a great policy or on a vote of confidence, failed to appeal to the country.   Then with a view to the enthusiasm of our friends in this country, as well as feeling in Ireland, it was essential that we should not let the flag go down. We had been constantly challenged to a dissolution, and not to take the challenge up would be a proof of mistrust, weakness, and a faint heart. ' My conclusion is ' he said ' a dissolution is formidable, but resignation would mean for the present juncture abandonment of the cause.'

Again Mr. Gladstone, who, as Lord Rosebery told the Queen " would never " resign " until he was beaten by the country," [77] wrote in his letter to Queen Victoria on June 8: [78]

Among the grounds of this advice (for dissolution) have been the evils of prolonged uncertainty upon an absorbing question, the likelihood of aggravated exasperation between sections and parties, the desirableness of maintaining a continuous action for the purpose of keeping Ireland the better in check and maintaining order there, and the obvious fairness of the argument, which has been and may be used without distinction of party (that) the opinion of the country should be constitutionally taken on a subject which is of vast importance, which was imperfectly before the body of Electors at the Last Election, and on which the Ministers of the Crown and the present representatives of the people are at variance.

Fnally, in the case of the dissolution of 1924, it may be

---

[76] Morley, *Life of Gladstone*, vol. iii, p. 341.

[77] *Letters of Queen Victoria, 1886-1901*, vol. i, p. 145.

[78] *Ibid.*, vol. i, pp. 143-144.

stated that, pending the vote in the House of Commons on October 8, the Labour Government had, two days before, decided on dissolution in the event of a defeat. Prime Minister MacDonald announced in the twenty-fourth Annual Conference of the Labour Party held in London on October 7 that " the country wishes us to go on with our work and not disturb and distract it yet with an election," but it " does not ask us to go on with our work under conditions that would lower the dignity of future Governments and cheapen the whole conception of the Cabinet." In case of defeat the situation would be such that " if we go, they (the Conservatives and the Liberals) will pretend that we have caused the election; if we stay, they will accuse us of being limpets on £5,000 a year (the salary of the First Lord of the Treasury." However, " if our Government had done everything of which it has been accused regarding the prosecution (the prosecution in the Campbell case), it could seek justification in what its predecessors have done." In Mr. MacDonald's view, a general election " will be caused by partisan abuse of Parliamentary votes, and the resentment against this chicanery . . . will make our victories all the more numerous when the country is allowed to judge our work. Some fresh, clean fighting in the constituencies may clear the air and gave us strength in the House of Commons which will make us independent of partisan interest." [79] The Labour Government's preference for a dissolution was more specifically alluded to when Mr. MacDonald said again in the Conference of the Labour Party on October 10, two days after the government's defeat, that: [80]

They (the combination of the Conservatives and the Liberals) knew that as soon as they did what they did last night, they had

[79] *Report of the Twenty-fourth Annual Conference of the Labour Party*, 1924, pp. 110-111.

[80] *Ibid.*, p. 183.

decreed that so far as this Parliament was concerned, its usefulness had gone. They knew perfectly well that this Parliament had already passed a vote of no confidence in Mr. Baldwin and his Party. They knew perfectly well that it was impossible for Mr. Baldwin and his Party to take up office again until that vote of no confidence had been rescinded. They knew perfectly well that, however much the Liberal Party might have liked to do in its heart, its numerical position put it not merely in the control of a combination, but put it in the control of either the Tory Party and (the word " or " was intended) ourselves, and that that Party was absolutely unthinkable as an alternative Government; and that the moment they, by this combination, passed the vote of censure on the Labour Government, then the Parliament was ended and there was nothing for it but to go to the country.

From the foregoing analysis, it may be inferred that dissolution was generally resorted to by a defeated government in preference to resignation for one or both of the following reasons: for the purpose of ascertaining the sentiments of the electorate in relation to some important issue of the time —as on the principle of free trade in 1841, parliamentary reform in 1859, disestablishment of the Irish Church in 1868 and Irish Home Rule in 1886 [81]—upon which the ministers of the Crown and the representatives of the people were at variance; or because of a conviction that the House of Commons, which had refused to give its confidence to the ministers of the Crown, did not correctly represent the opinions and wishes of the nation, and an expectation that a more favorable House of Commons would be returned as a result of a General Election—as in 1857, 1859, 1868, 1886 and 1924. It must of course be recognized that the dissolution of 1868 was also in part an automatic consequence of the extension of the suffrage in 1867 and that those in

[81] See *supra*, pp. 104-106.

1857 and 1868 were partly due to the influence of the sovereign. The dissolution of 1841 stands out as the only case in which a Prime Minister, confronted with adverse by-election returns and doubtful of the success of an appeal to the nation, after his defeat in the House of Commons ever advised a dissolution, on account of the necessity of maintaining the principle of Cabinet solidarity.[82] As for the other five dissolutions—those in 1857, 1859, 1868, 1886 and 1924—it should be further emphasized that since the Opposition which defeated the government on each of those occasions did not itself enjoy the confidence of the House of Commons and since the government formed by it had resigned as a result of defeat previously registered in the House of Commons,[83] the difficulty in forming another gov-

---

[82] It may be of some interest to cite here the frequently cited anecdote of Lord Melbourne:

" ... early in February (1841), Lord John (Russell) formally brought before the Cabinet the question of corn. In the two months which followed, representations were made to the Government that frauds had been and always would be committed while a sliding scale was continued; and the Cabinet consequently determined to substitute a fixed duty of 8s. on wheat for the graduated duty which Lord John had originally suggested. Some members of the Cabinet, indeed, had little enthusiasm for the change; and the Prime Minister himself, as his colleagues were leaving the room, said, ' By the bye, there is one thing we haven't agreed upon, which is, what we are to say. Is it to make our corn dearer or cheaper or to make the price steady? I don't care which; but we had better all be in the same story.' " Walpole, *Life of Lord John Russell*, vol. i, p. 369.

[83]

Parliament	Ministries defeated by	Result of such defeat
1852-1857	1. Lord Derby's	Resignation
	2. Lord Aberdeen's	Resignation
	3. Lord Palmerston's	Dissolution
1857-1859	1. Lord Palmerston's	Resignation
	2. Lord Derby's	Dissolution
1865-1868	1. Lord Russell's	Resignation
	2. Mr. Disraeli's	Dissolution
1885-1886	1. Lord Salisbury's	Resignation
	2. Mr. Gladstone's	Dissolution
1923-1924	1. Mr. Baldwin's	Resignation
	2. Mr. MacDonald's	Dissolution

ernment by the Opposition, necessarily inherent in government under a two-party system of the English type,[84] provided a strong argument for resort to a dissolution of Parliament by the newly-defeated ministry instead of relinquishing the offices held.

Since preference for dissolution after a defeat in the House of Commons was based largely upon the desire of gaining seats in the new House, it may be interesting to examine the actual result of appeals to the nation in the above six cases. Except in the case of 1857, the vote of the nation was, contrary to what had been said by the heads of the defeated government pending the vote of the electorate, a decisive disapproval of the government.[85]   Consequently, the government, since another dissolution was not possible, had no other choice but to resign—as did the Melbourne Ministry in

It should be remarked here that only in one case did a government in which the House of Commons had previously expressed its lack of confidence face the same House again after the resignation of the government formed by the opposite party because of defeat in the same House. But this government—the government formed by Lord Salisbury in 1895 —immediately upon its assumption of office advised a dissolution and appealed to the nation for support. *Supra*, pp. 79-80.

[84] The situation would, of course, be quite different under a parliamentary system like that of France.   There the existence of many parties and the absence of strong party discipline has, at least up to the present and since 1877, always made it possible to find an alternative to a defeated government in the same Chamber.

[85] The returns of the General Elections were as follows:

1841	Conservatives	368	Liberals	289
1857	"	281	"	373
1859	"	307	"	347
1868	"	279	"	379
1886	"		316; Liberal Unionists, 78; Gladstonian Liberals, 191; Nationalists, 85.	
1924	Conservatives, 412; Socialist, 151; Liberal, 40; Constitutional, 7; Independent, 5.			

The Constitutional Year Book, 1933, pp. 255-256.

August, 1841 [86] and the Derby Ministry in June, 1859 [87] as a result of defeat in the new House of Commons on the Address in answer to the Speech from the Throne, and the Disraeli Ministry in December, 1868, [88] the Gladstone Ministry in July, 1886 [89] and the MacDonald Ministry in November, 1924 [90] as a direct result of the General Elections. All these facts tend to support the following statement made by Alpheus Todd at the end of the last century: [91]

> The verdict of the House of Commons . . . derives its strength and efficacy from its being a true reflex of the intelligent will of the whole community. Until a vote of the Commons has been ratified by the constituent body, it will seldom be regarded as conclusively determining upon the existence of a ministry.

We have discussed resignation and dissolution, the alternatives in case of defeat, and the verdict of the electorate, should a defeated government prefer a dissolution to a resignation, as a determining factor in the fate of government. Now, if a more exhaustive study of the interrelation between resignation and dissolution is to be pursued, attention ought to be directed to the question as to how far resignation and dissolution, irrespective of the existence of any cause that might have brought about either of such courses, may have interacted—that is, how often a dissolution of Parliament came about through a change of ministry and how often the ministry fell through the employment of dissolution—and the

[86] 59 *Hansard* (Commons) 3 s., 342-455, 475-479; 59 *Hansard* (Lords) 3 s., 473-474.

[87] 154 *Hansard* (Commons) 3 s., 297-421, 431; 154 *Hansard* (Lords) 3 s., 423-427.

[88] Monypenny and Buckle, *Life of Disraeli*, vol. v, pp. 93-96.

[89] Morley, *Life of Gladstone*, vol. iii, pp. 345-347.

[90] *Annual Register*, 1924, English History, p. 118.

[91] Todd, *On Parliamentary Government in England*, vol. ii, p. 485.

constitutional significance of such an interaction. So far as we can gather, there were, during the period under discussion, seven occasions on which a newly appointed Prime Minister, whatever the cause of his accession to power might have been, submitted a choice of ministries to the electorate upon his assumption of office. While decision of the people in the first three of the seven cases, that is, in 1834, 1852 and 1885, was decidedly against the new appointment, those of 1895, 1906, 1922 and 1931 gave undoubted approval to the change of Ministry.[92] When the new House of Commons had expressed its lack of confidence—in the Peel Ministry in 1835 (through a series of defeats including an Amendment to the Address censuring the government on dissolution to which reference has already been made) [93] in the Derby Min-

[92] The returns of the General Elections were as follows:

1834	....	Conservatives 275	Liberals 383		
1852	....	" 331	" 323		
1885	....	" 250	" 334; Nationalists, 86.		
1895	....	" 341; Liberal Unionists, 70; Gladstonian Liberals, 177; Nationalists, 82.			
1906	....	Conservatives, 134; Liberal Unionists, 23; Liberals, 376; Laborites, 54; Nationalists, 83.			
1922	....	Conservatives, 344; National Liberal, 53; Independent Liberal, 61; Labor, 142; Independent, 12; Nationalist, 2; Sinn Fein, 1.			
1931	....	Conservative, 469; National, 4; Liberal, 33; National Liberal, 35; National Labor, 13; Labor, 52; Independent Liberal, 4; Independent, 5.			

(*The Constitutional Year Book*, 1933, pp. 255-256.)
Of the 331 " Conservative " members in the Parliament elected in 1852, only 310 were, as Lord Derby said in the House of Lords on December 20, 1852, " the supporters of the Government, on questions not involving the question of free trade or a protective policy, but ... parties who were generally disposed to give their confidence to Her Majesty's Ministers." 123 *Hansard* (Lords) 3 s., 1698-1705.

[93] The defeats sustained by the Peel Government in 1835 and the majorities against it on those divisions are as follows:

istry in December, 1852 on the Budget[94] and in the Salisbury Ministry in January, 1886 on the Address[95]—the ministry involved, since another dissolution was out of the question in each case, tendered its resignation to the sovereign.[96] On the other hand, the ministries of 1895, 1906, 1922 and 1931, as a result of success in the General Election, were granted a new lease of life.

With regard to resignations of ministries due to the dissolution of Parliament and loss of support in the country in general, it may be said, in supplement to what has already been pointed out, that since the Reform of 1832 there have been thirteen such cases, in seven of which—that is, in 1835,

February	19	On choice of Speaker	10: 306 vs. 316
February	26	On the Address	7: 302 vs. 309
March	26	On the Motion for an Address to his Majesty to grant a charter to the London University	110 136 vs. 246
April	2	On Lord John Russell's Resolution relative to the Church of Ireland	33: 289 vs. 321
April	7	On Lord John Russell's Resolution relating to the Church of Ireland in a Committee of the whole House	25: 237 vs. 262
April	7	On Lord John Russell's second Resolution on bringing up the Report of the Committee relative to Irish Tithes	27: 258 vs. 285

26 *Hansard* (Commons) 3 s., 56-61, 410-415; 27 *Hanasrd* (Commons) 3 s., 301-303, 772-777, 861-864, 969-974.

[94] 123 *Hansard* (Commons) 3 s., 1569-1597.

[95] 302 *Hansard* (Commons) 3 s., 442-530.

[96] 1835: 27 *Hansard* (Lords) 3 s., 974.
          27 *Hansard* (Commons) 3 s., 980-984.
    1852: 123 *Hansard* (Lords) 3 s., 1698-1705.
          123 *Hansard* (Commons) 3 s., 1709-1710.
    1886: 302 *Hansard* (Lords) 3 s., 531, 533-4.
          302 *Hansard* (Commons) 3 s., 532-3, 534.

1841, 1852, 1859, 1886 (Lord Salisbury), 1892, and 1924 (Baldwin)—the ministry resigned only when the lack of confidence on the part of the people had been further confirmed through a vote by their representatives in Parliament. In 1868 when the Disraeli Government, as has been said, after having been defeated in Parliament had appealed from Parliament to the country and had failed to secure the support of the people, the Prime Minister, who had, twenty-seven years before, criticized, from the Opposition bench, the then existing government for remaining in office and meeting Parliament as if nothing had happened, thought it advisable, under a similar situation, to discard the precedent which he had condemned as a policy resting on constitutional fictions and not on facts. He accordingly acknowledged the reality and resigned without meeting Parliament.[97] The precedent thus set was followed by Gladstone in 1874 [98] and 1886, by Lord Beaconsfield (formerly Mr. Disraeli) himself in 1880,[99] by MacDonald in 1924 and Baldwin in 1929, although in 1886 and 1929 the verdict of the election, while clearly against the government, did not yield an independent or absolute majority for any other party.[100] In 1885 and 1892 Lord Salisbury

[97] Monypenny and Buckle, *Life of Disraeli*, vol. ii, p. 116; vol. v, pp. 93-4.

[98] Morley, *Life of Gladstone*, vol. ii, pp. 492-493.

[99] Monypenny and Buckle, *op. cit.*, vol. vi, p. 536.

[100] The considerations that guided Mr. Gladstone in deciding for resignation in 1886 were, as Morley said, as follows: " It is best for Ireland that the Party strongest in the new parliament should be at once confronted with its responsibilities. Again, we were bound to consider what would most tend to reunite the liberal party, and it was in opposition that the chances of such union would be likely to stand highest, especially in view of coercion which many of the dissidents had refused to contemplate. If he could remodel the bill (the Irish Home Rule Bill) or frame a new one, that might be a possible ground for endeavouring to make up a majority, but he could not see his way to any such process, though he was ready for certain amendments. Finally, if we remained,

and in 1923 Mr. Baldwin took a different course on the ground that, though there was probably a majority against the ministers, it was not a homogeneous majority and might fairly be tested in Parliament; but the government did not survive the Address on any of these occasions.[101] The conclusion drawn from these incidents by Cecil S. Emden [102] may be restated as follows: while the people's verdict in a General Election from 1841 onwards come to be talked of as the determining factor in the choice of the Ministry, it was, in all clear cases, absolute in and after 1868. If the facts regarding dissolutions, brought about by newly appointed ministries are taken into consideration, the further generalization may be advanced that, with some exceptions, since 1868 a change of ministry has been the result of a General Election or has immediately received the ratification of such an election.[103] Thus, dissolution, though theoretically " an instrument of the Crown," has been used by ministers not only in solving deadlocks between themselves and the majority of the representatives of the people, but also in deciding the fate of the government, and especially, during recent years, in ratifying a change of ministry.

an amendment would be moved definitely committing the new House against home rule." Morley, *op. cit.*, vol. iii, pp. 346-347.

After the General Election of 1929, " Mr. Baldwin might have remained in office, as he had done in 1923, till it was confirmed by Parliament; and so he was advised to do by some of his colleagues, in order, as they said, that the Liberals might have the responsibility of putting the Socialists in office. Mr. Baldwin, however, preferred to bow to the plain intention of the majority of the electorate, and on June 4, he placed his resignation in the hands of the King." *Annual Register*, 1929, English History, p. 47.

[101] Concerning the resignations of 1886 and 1892, see *supra*, p. 155, fn. 95 and p. 79, fn. 45.

For Mr. Baldwin's defeat and his announcement of resignation in the House of Commons, *cf.* 169 *H. C. Deb.* 5 s., 587-686, 703, and 56 *H. L. Deb.* 5 s., 70.

[102] Emden, *The People and the Constitution*, p. 162.

[103] *Cf.* Lowell, *The Government of England*, vol. i, pp. 437-438.

In our discussion of the interrelation between resignation and dissolution, we have touched upon the various causes that led to a great many resignations. The analysis in the preceding pages shows that during the hundred-year period since the Reform of 1832, there have been, aside from the changes of government on five occasions due either to the death or the ill-health of the Prime Minister, one case of dismissal by the sovereign, ten cases of resignations because of government defeats in the House of Commons and thirteen cases of change of government which were the result of General Elections. In some of these thirteen cases the government did not even wait to meet the newly-chosen House of Commons. For our purpose here it must suffice to add that of the remaining eight cases among the thirty-seven, five (Grey's Cabinet in 1834,[104] Peel's in 1845,[105] Gladstone's in 1894,[106] Balfour's in 1905,[107] and Asquith's in 1916 [108]) were produced by a break-up of the Cabinet, one (Lloyd George's in 1922) [109] by a party vote and one (Asquith's in 1915) [110] by the necessity of reorganizing the government to cope with unusual problems that had arisen. The last of the eight cases (MacDonald in 1931) [111] was

[104] Cf. 24 Hansard (Lords) 3 s., 1305-1311; 24 Hansard (Commons) 3 s., 1335-1338; Trevelyan, Lord Grey of the Reform Bill (London, 1920), pp. 391-2.

[105] Cf. Memoirs by Sir Robert Peel, vol. ii, pp. 97 et seq., esp. 221-2; Sir Robert Peel from his Private Papers, vol. iii, pp. 222-243.

[106] Cf. Morley, Recollections, vol. ii, pp. 3-10; Crewe, Lord Rosebery, pp. 356-361.

[107] See supra, p. 80.

[108] Cf. Earl of Oxford and Asquith, Memories and Reflections, 1852-1927, vol. ii, pp. 152-178; Lord Newton, Lord Lansdowne (London, 1929), pp. 452-455.

[109] See supra, pp. 88-89.

[110] Cf. 72 H. C. Deb. 5 s., 557-561; Earl of Oxford and Asquith, op. cit., vol. ii, pp. 114-116.

[111] See supra, pp. 90-92.

characterized both by a split in the Cabinet and by the apparent necessity of reorganization to cope with the difficulties arising out of economic crisis. Taking these resignations in chronological order we may therefore conclude, as did Sir William Anson in 1907, that "in the last hundred years the power which determines the existence and extinction of (the) Cabinet has shifted, first from the Crown to the Commons and then from The Commons to the electorate"[112] and (what Anson failed to mention) to the political parties. But, in case of withdrawal of confidence by the House of Commons, there always exists a theoretical alternative to resignation. On seven occasions (in 1836, 1841, 1852, 1859, 1886, 1892 and 1924), however, when the vote of the House of Commons amounted to nothing more than a register of the government's defeat at a recent General Election, the alternative of dissolution was evidently not available. On the other sixteen occasions, when free choice between resignation and dissolution might have been made, decision upon one course of action in preference to another (resignation being preferred in 1839, 1846, 1851, 1852, 1855, 1858, 1866, 1873, 1885, and 1895 and dissolution in 1841, 1857, 1859, 1868, 1886, and 1924) depended in general very much upon the sentiment of the country, sometimes clearly manifested in the returns of by-elections, and also upon the cohesion of the party in power. In view of this fact and in consideration also of recent practice on the part of the ministry of resigning immediately after a General Election or as a direct result of a party vote and the practice of a newly appointed ministry in appealing to the nation for support, the principle seems established that the ministry is "answerable immediately to the majority of the House of Commons, and ultimately to the electors whose will creates that majority"[113] and, to a

---

[112] Anson, *The Law and Custom of the Constitution*, vol. ii, pp. 133-134.
[113] See *supra*, p. 17, fn. 16.

certain extent, to the political party by which the ministry is formed. In matters concerning confidence and office, the electorate has, since the memorable resignation of Disraeli in 1868 which was regarded by Spencer Walpole as " the first open recognition in history that the House of Commons itself was of less importance than the electorate," [114] become more and more influential, while the wire-pulling of political parties, the ever controlling factor behind the scenes in the House of Commons, has also, since the Eighteen Seventies, become more and more dominant. So far as these matters are concerned, the "centre of gravity" in the House of Commons (to use one of Professor Laski's phrases) [115] now lies beyond the reach of the voices of its most eloquent members. In the House of Commons where, since the regulation of debates, the maximum amount of noise can no longer be made, only a minimum amount of harm has been done to the ministry.

[114] Walpole, *History of Twenty-five years* (London, 1908), vol. ii, p. 347.

[115] Laski, *Democracy in Crisis* (University of N. C. Press, 1933), pp. 91-2.

CHAPTER VI

CONCLUSION

IN the preceding analysis of the different phases of the problem of the dissolution of Parliament and its relation to the resignation of the ministry, we have laid considerable emphasis on the idea of ministerial responsibility. From our point of view the constitutional significance of the prerogative of dissolution lies chiefly in its being exercised as a complementary power to ministerial responsibility to the House of Commons in English parliamentary government. With respect to the establishment of such responsibility we have said that the prerogative of dissolution has, since the beginning of the eighteenth century, never been exercised by the king without ministerial advice,[1] and the practice followed by the sovereign of announcing dissolution in person in the House of Lords was, at about that time, superseded by the issuance, following the prorogation of Parliament in the House of Lords, of a Royal Proclamation by the King " by and with the advice of his Privy Council." [2] Except through his dismissal of ministers who had majority support in the House of Commons, dissolution was not precipitated by any action on the part of the sovereign. Although since 1834, the last time that a ministry was dismissed,[3] the wearer of the English Crown has more than once suggested and pressed for a dissolution, no Parliament has been dissolved solely because of the influence of the sovereign.[4] Nor has the

[1] *Cf. supra,* p. 16.
[2] *Cf. supra,* pp. 16-17.
[3] *Cf. supra,* pp. 43-45.
[4] *Cf. supra,* pp. 45-54.

sovereign been able to refuse dissolution, when advised by
the Prime Minister as was shown in 1858, when dissolution
was advised by Lord Derby.[5]   By the middle of the nineteenth century, when the sovereign abstained from the prorogation ceremony in the House of Lords,[6] it had become an
established fact that the power of dissolution, though one
of the king's prerogatives, is exercised not by the king himself but by his ministers in his name.   When a dissolution
is not advised, he can hardly be successful in pressing for
one;[7] when it is advised, he will no longer refuse.[8]   In the
exercise of this prerogative, the king's person is symbolized
by a Royal Commission during the prorogation in the House
of Lords, and his will and pleasure to dissolve one Parliament
and to call another is embodied in a Royal Proclamation
issued on ministerial advice.

It has been seen that advice on dissolution is usually
given by the Prime Minister with the consent of the Cabinet.[9]
Hence, by giving such advice to the sovereign, the ministers
as a body incur responsibility to the House of Commons.[10]
Since the establishment of the principles of Cabinet solidarity
and ministerial responsibility for legislation the ministers
have been held jointly responsible on all important measures
and policies, including the question of dissolution itself.   The
enforcement of this responsibility, through the withdrawal
of confidence, usually leads, so far as the constitutional practice of the nineteenth century is concerned, either to a resignation of the ministry or to the dissolution of Parliament.[11]

[5] *Cf. supra*, pp. 54-55.

[6] *Cf. supra*, pp. 117-119.

[7] *Cf. supra*, pp. 45-54.

[8] Laski, Harold J., "The Position of Parties and the Right of Dissolution," *Fabian Tracts*, no. 210, March, 1924. And *cf. supra*, pp. 39-43.

[9] *Cf. supra*, pp. 28-34.

[10] *Cf. supra*, pp. 33-34, 60-61.

[11] *Cf. supra*, pp. 70-82, 127, fn. 13.

On the other hand, the ministry may, in these days of paid members and expensive elections, through a threat of dissolution, secure Parliamentary support and efficiency in carrying on the work of the House of Commons.[12]

In case of withdrawal of confidence by the House of Commons, the defeated ministry, in making its choice between resignation and dissolution, usually takes into consideration not only the general attitude of the electorate, sometimes clearly indicated in the by-election returns, but also the probability of support by the members of the party.[13] Between 1832 and 1868, however, no matter how clearly the attitude of the electorate was indicated in by-elections or in a General Election, the ministry in such cases always waited for a defeat on a vote in the House of Commons before resigning or (if circumstances permitted) moving towards a dissolution. Similarly in this period neither shifts in party alignment, no matter how evident to all observers, nor party decisions taken outside the House, induced any ministry to resign or dissolve before these changes in the political situation had produced a vote in the House of Commons adverse to the Cabinet.[14]

But since 1868, and especially since 1900, the "centre of gravity" in English politics has shifted from the House of Commons itself to the Cabinet, parties and the people. The Cabinet exercises a strong control over the representative assembly, almost monopolizing the time of the House and depriving the private members of legislative initiative.[15] Party organization has grown more rigid with the extension of the suffrage, and the lines of party control over members

[12] *Cf. supra*, pp. 54-57, 69, fn. 126.

[13] *Cf. supra*, pp. 127-152.

[14] *Cf. supra*, pp. 83-85, 158-160.

[15] *Cf.* Muir, *How Britain is Governed* (New York, 1930), pp. 87-91.

of Parliament have tightened accordingly.[16]   Meanwhile the people themselves have come to assume a more important place in the process of government, a tendency clearly indicated by the growth of the idea of mandate.[17]

Such important developments have been accompanied, naturally enough, by corresponding changes both in the practice of resignation and in the use of the power of dissolution. Thus we now find the ministry tending to relinquish office immediately after an unfavorable General Election or as a direct result of a party vote while the power of dissolution, formerly used by ministers chiefly to solve deadlocks between themselves and the elected representatives of the people, is now employed chiefly to secure popular ratification of a change of ministry, to secure a popular mandate on a specific policy, or to secure the decision of the ultimate sovereign on the fate of the government.   The power of dissolution thus remains an important element in the responsible government of England, but the impulse to its use comes less often than formerly from acts or decisions within the House of Commons, more often from acts or decisions of outside agencies or from a regard to the will of the sovereign people.

[16] *Cf. ibid.,* pp. 120-126.   Ostrogorski, *Democracy and the Organization of Political Parties* (New York, 1902), vol. i, second part, 9th chapter.

[17] *Cf. supra,* pp. 103-108, 159-160.   Emden, *The People and the Constitution,* pp. 168 *et seq.*

BIBLIOGRAPHY

I

STATUTES, PARLIAMENTARY DEBATES AND JOURNALS OF PARLIAMENT

The Statutes at Large, 1100-1865, 105 vols.
The Public General Statutes, 1866-1932, 70 vols.
Adams, George B. and Stephens, H. M., *Select Documents of English Constitutional History*, New York, 1901.
Dykes, D. O., *Source Book of Constitutional History from 1660*, London, 1930.
Parliamentary History of England, vol. 23.
Hansard Parliamentary Debates, 3rd ser., 1830-1891, 350 vols.
Hansard Parliamentary Debates, 4th ser., 1892-1908, 77 vols.
House of Commons Debates (H. C. Deb.), 5th ser., 1909 to date.
House of Lords Debates (H. L. Deb.), 5th ser., 1909 to date.
Journals of the House of Lords, vols. 64, 66, 86, 99, 100, 105, 117, 154 and 163.
Journals of the House of Commons, vols. 155, 161 and 165.

II

LETTERS, PAPERS, MEMOIRS AND BIOGRAPHIES

Ashley, Evelyn, *Life of Viscount Palmerston*, London, 1876, 2 vols.
The Earl of Oxford and Asquith, *Fifty Years of British Parliament*, Boston, 1926, 2 vols.
——, *Memories and Reflections, 1852-1927*, Boston, 1928, 2 vols.
Duke of Buckingham and Chandos, *Memoirs of the Courts and Cabinets of William IV and Victoria*, London, 1861, 2 vols.
Cecil, Lady Gwendolen, *Life of Robert Marquis of Salisbury*, London, 1922-32, 4 vols.
Churchill, Winston S., *Lord Randolph Churchill*, New York, 1906, 2 vols.
——, *A Roving Commission, My Early Life*, New York, 1930.
——, *The World Crisis, the Aftermath*, London, 1929.
Clark, George K., *Peel and the Conservative Party*, London, 1929.
Marquess of Crewe, *Lord Rosebery*, New York, 1931.
The Croker Papers, ed. by Louis J. Jennings, London, 1884, 3 vols.
Dasent, A. I., *John Thadeus Delane, His Life and Correspondence*, New York, 1908, 2 vols.
Elliot, Arthur D., *Life of Lord Goschen*, London, 1911, 2 vols.

165

Fiscal Reform, Speeches delivered by A. J. Balfour from June 1880 to December 1905, London, 1906.

Fitzroy, Sir Almeric, *Memoirs*, London, 5th edi, 2 vols.

Gardiner, A. G., *Life of Sir William Harcourt*, London, 1923, 2 vols.

Gathorne Hardy, First Earl of Cranbrook, A Memoir, edi. by Alfred E. Gathorne Hardy, London, 1910, 2 vols.

The Greville Memoirs, A Journal of the Reigns of King George IV and King William IV, ed. by Henry Reeve, London, 1875, 3 vols.

——, *1837-1852*, ed. by Henry Reeve, London, 1885, 3 vols.

——, *1852-1860*, ed. by Henry Reeve, London, 1887, 2 vols.

Viscount Grey, *Twenty-Five Years, 1892-1916*, New York, 1925, 2 vols.

Griffith-Boscawen, A. S. T., *Fourteen Years in Parliament*, London, 1907.

Holland, Bernard, *Life of Spencer Compton, Eighth Duke of Devonshire*, London, 1911, 2 vols.

Lee, Sidney, *King Edward VII*, London, 1925-1927, 2 vols.

Lowther, James, W., *A Speaker's Commentaries*, London, 1925, 2 vols.

Lucy, Henry W., *A Diary of Two Parliaments, 1874-1885*, London, 1885-1886, 2 vols.

——, *A Diary of the Salisbury Parliament, 1886-1892*, London, 1892.

——, *A Diary of the Home Rule Parliament, 1892-1895*, London, 1896.

——, *A Diary of the Unionist Parliament, 1895-1900*, Bristol, 1901.

——, *The Balfourian Parliament, 1900-1905*, London, 1906.

Martin, Theodore, *Life of the Prince Consort*, London, 1875-1880, 5 vols.

Maxwell, Sir Herbert, *Life and Letters of the Fourth Earl of Clarendon*, London, 1913, 2 vols.

——, *Life of Wellington*, London, 1899, 2 vols.

Lord Melbourne's Papers, ed. by Lloyd C. Sanders, London, 1889.

Monypenny, William F. and Buckle, George E., *Life of Benjamin Disraeli*, London, 1910-1920, 6 vols.

Morley, John, *Life of William E. Gladstone*, New York, 1903, 3 vols.

——, *Recollections*, New York, 1917, 2 vols.

The Works of Lord Morley, London, 1921, vol. xiii, *Walpole*.

Lord Newton, *Lord Lansdowne*, London, 1929.

Memoirs by Sir Robert Peel, published by Lord Mahon and Edward Cardwell, London, 1856-1857, 2 vols.

Sir Robert Peel, From His Private Papers, ed. by Charles S. Parker, London, 1891-1899, 3 vols.

Ponsonby, Sir Frederick, *Side Lights on Queen Victoria*, New York, 1930.

Raymond, E. T., *Mr. Balfour, A Biography*, London, 1920.

——, *Life of Lord Rosebery*, New York, 1923.

Earl of Ronaldshay, *Life of Lord Curzon*, New York, 1927, 3 vols.

Lord Rosebery, *Pitt*, London, 1919.

Lord Russell, *Recollections and Suggestions, 1813-1873*, London, 1875.

Early Correspondence of Lord John Russell, 1805-1840, ed. by Rollo Russell, London, 1913, 2 vols.

Later Correspondence of Lord John Russell, 1840-1878, ed. by G. P. Gooch, New York, 1925, 2 vols.

Earl of Selborne, *Memorials,* Part I, Family and Personal, 1766-1865, London, 1896, 2 vols.; Part II, Personal and Political, 1865-1895, London, 1898, 2 vols.

Spender, J. A., *Life of Sir Henry Campbell-Bannerman,* London, 1923, 2 vols.

Memoirs of Baron Stockmar, by his son Baron E. von Stockmar, tr. from the German by G. A. M. and ed. by F. Max Muller, London, 1873, 2 vols.

Strachey, Lytton, *Queen Victoria,* New York, 1931.

Thursfield, J. R., *Peel,* London, 1904.

Tiltman, H. H., *James Ramsay MacDonald, Labour's Man of Destiny,* 4th ed., London.

Torrens, W. M., *Memoirs of Viscount Melbourne,* London, 1878, 2 vols.

Trevelyan, George M., *Lord Grey of the Reform Bill,* London, 1920.

Letters of Queen Victoria, 1837-1861, ed. by A. C. Benson and Viscount Esher, New York, 1907, 3 vols.

——, *1862-1885,* ed. by George E. Buckle, New York, 1926-1928, 3 vols.

——, *1886-1901,* ed. by George E. Buckle, New York, 1930-1932, 3 vols.

Walpole, Sir Spencer, *History of Twenty-Five Years,* 1856-1880, London, 1908, 4 vols.

——, *Life of Lord John Russell,* London, 1889, 2 vols.

Whates, H., *The Third Salisbury Administration, 1895-1900,* Westminster, undated.

Wolf, Lucien, *Life of Lord Ripon,* London, 1921, 2 vols.

III

COMMENTARIES AND TREATISES

Adams, George B., *Constitutional History of England,* New York, 1921.

Allyn, Emily, *Lords Versus Commons,* Philadelphia, 1931.

Anson, Sir William, *The Law and Custom of the Constitution,* vol. i, 4th edition, Oxford, 1909; vol. ii, 3rd ed., Oxford, 1907 and vol. iii, 3rd ed., Oxford, 1908. Also 5th ed., Oxford, 1922, 3 vols.

Bagehot, Walter, *The English Constitution,* New York and London, 1927.

Courtney, Leonard, *The Working Constitution of the United Kingdom,* New York, 1910.

Dicey, A. V., *Introduction to the Study of the Law of the Constitution,* London, 1889.

Emden, Cecil S., *The People and the Constitution,* Oxford, 1933.

Green, John R., *A Short History of the English People,* New York, 2nd edition.

Hallam, Henry, *The Constitutional History of England*, London, 1832, 3 vols.

Ilbert, Sir Courtenay, *Parliament*, New York and London, 1911.

Laski, Harold J., *The Crisis and the Constitution: 1931 and after*, London, 1932.

——, *Democracy in Crisis*, University of N. C. Press, 1933.

Low, Sidney, *The Governance of England*, London, 1904.

Lowell, A. Lawrence, *The Government of England*, New York, 1919, 2 vols.

McBain, H. E. and Rogers, L., *The New Constitutions of Europe*, Garden City, New York, 1923.

MacDonagh, Michael, *The Book of Parliament*, London, 1897.

——, *The English King*, New York, 1929.

——, *The Pageant of Parliament*, London, 1921, 2 vols.

May, Thomas E., *The Constitutional History of England*, Boston, 1862, 2 vols.

May, Thomas E. and Holland, Francis, *The Constitutional History of England*, London, 1912, vol. iii.

Muir, Ramsay, *How Britain is Governed*, New York, 1930.

Ogg, F. A., *English Government and Politics*, New York, 1930.

Ostrogorski, M., *Democracy and the Organization of Political Parties*, trans. from the French by Frederick Clarke, New York, 1902.

Pollard, A. F., *The Evolution of Parliament*, London, 1926.

Redlich, Josef, *The Procedure of the House of Commons*, tr. from the German by A. E. Steinthal, London, 1908, 3 vols.

Sait, E. M. and Barrows, D. P., *British Politics in Transition*, Yonkers-on-Hudson, N. Y., 1925.

Todd, Alpheus, *On Parliamentary Government in England*, London, 1887-89, 2 vols.

IV

MAGAZINE ARTICLES

Laski, Harold J., "The Position of Parties and the Right of Dissolution", *Fabian Tract*, no. 210, March, 1924.

Marriott, J. A. R., "The Answer of Demos," *The Fortnightly Review*, vol. 121, pp. 105-117, January, 1924; vol. 132, pp. 10-18, July, 1929 and vol. 136, pp. 681-692, December, 1931.

——, "Cabinet Government—Its Future?", *The Fortnightly Review*, vol. 137, pp. 311-322, March, 1932.

——, "The Crown and the Crisis," *The Fortnightly Review*, vol. 96, pp. 448-492, Sept., 1911 and vol. 136, pp. 579-589, Nov., 1931.

——, "The 'Mystery' of the Monarchy," *The Fortnightly Review*, vol. 134, pp. 770-783, Dec., 1930.

Masterman, C. F. G., "The Dissolution," *Contemporary Review,* vol. 126, pp. 544-552, Nov., 1924.

Morgan, J. H., "The King and His Prerogative," *The Nineteenth Century and After,* vol. 70, pp. 215-225, Aug., 1911.

Randall, J. G., "The Frequency and Duration of Parliament", *American Political Science Review,* vol. x, no. 4, Nov., 1916.

Rogers, Lindsay, "The Changing English Constitution," *The North American Review,* vol. 219, pp. 758-768, June, 1924.

——, "Aspects of German Political Institutions," *Political Science Quarterly,* vol. xlvii, no. 3, Sept., 1932.

——, "Ministerial Instability in France," *Political Science Quarterly,* vol. xlvi, no. 1, March, 1931.

——, "Parliamentary Commissions, in France, II," *Political Science Quarterly,* vol. xxxviii, no. 4, Dec., 1923.

Samuel, Sir Herbert, "The Device of the Referendum," *The Nation and Athenæum,* vol. 46, pp. 791-792, March 15, 1930.

Strachey, J. St. Loe, "A Minority Premier," *Spectator,* vol. 131, p. 1020, December 29, 1923.

Swift MacNeill, J. G., "The Prime Minister and the Prerogative of Dissolution," *The Fortnightly Review,* vol. 117, pp. 747-753, May, 1922.

"The Prerogative of Dissolution," *Round Table,* vol. 20, no. 77, pp. 32-49, Dec., 1929.

V

YEARBOOKS, NEWSPAPERS, ETC.

Annual Register, 1841, 1847, 1873, 1895, 1922, 1923, 1924, 1929 and 1931.

Constitutional Year Book, 1924, 1932 and 1933.

Report of the Twenty-Fourth Annual Conference of the Labour Party, 1924.

The Liberal Magazine, Nov., 1922 and Nov., 1924.

The Liberal Yearbook, 1930 and 1932.

The Times (London), Nov. 11, 1910; Nov. 18, 1918; Oct. 27, 1922; Oct. 26 and Nov. 9, 1923; Oct. 7 and 10, 1924; Aug. 24, Aug. 26 and Oct. 8, 1931.

The New York Times, Nov. 14, 1923.

INDEX